I0680838

THE HELICON WEST ANTHOLOGY

A Ten-Year Celebration of Featured Readers

Edited by
Star Coulbrooke
with
Tim Keller
and
Chadd VanZanten

Helicon West Press
Logan Utah
2016

Copyright © by Helicon West Press

Printed in the United States of America

Editors: Star Coulbrooke, Tim Keller, and Chadd VanZanten
Cover art: Mallory Culley
Book design: Maria Williams

ISBN-13: 978-0997744408
First Edition

PRODUCTION MADE POSSIBLE

Production of this anthology was made possible by many generous donors:

Premier Patrons ($100-$1000)

USU CHaSS Dean's Office (John Allen, Dean of the College)
Utah Humanities Council
Val and Brenda Laws
Anonymous

Patrons ($50)

Jordon Roberts
Logan Library
Taylor Brown
Lisa Roullard
Amanda Luzzader
Karen Erickson
Blake Sleight
Jenava Tait
Nano Taggart
Steve Shively
Star Coulbrooke
Justin Young
Charles Waugh
Nandini Vayas
Lauren Scholnick
Mary Ellen Greenwood
Christopher Cokinos
Jack Remick
Bill Trowbridge

Friends ($18-$30)

Although not listed here by name, friends will receive a signed complimentary copy of the anthology.

Sincere thanks to all who gave. We couldn't have done it without you.

CONTENTS

Slam Poetry and Flash Prose

INTRODUCTION

Helicon West is a reading series that began in a spare conference room at Utah State University and moved to a small café in downtown Logan, where it grew out of that and its next two venues to become the literary cornerstone of Utah. I'm not exaggerating. Since January 2006, poets laureate and published authors of other genres have graced the Helicon West podium. The audiences they enjoy are consistently larger than in other non-academic reading series around the state and in most areas of the West. Aspiring writers of every stripe have clamored to appear at the twice-monthly Helicon West open microphone after being inspired by featured authors from all over the country. This anthology is a celebration of the first ten years of readings, with selections from fifty-nine of the featured authors.

It begins with Dinty W. Moore's short memoir titled "You Know Better," which slices into one of those mistakes we make as children when our underdeveloped sense of reason justifies actions we will come to regret more deeply than we did at the time we were called-out for the transgression. Moore is an expert at understatement, a Buddhist memoirist. I felt myself cringing psychologically as I read this deceptively simple story, remembering childhood lessons that I've had to apply over and over as I've aged.

Age and the acquisition of knowledge. Katharine Coles, former Poet Laureate of Utah, follows the Moore piece with a set of poems on that paired theme.

Then there are the questions of the body.
What holds it together? What falls
Apart? All of us are faltering, all
In our own ways going rough and shoddy:

Coles' poetry topics are diverse and erudite, grounded in science, generous in spirit. In this volume are seven poems about aging dogs, poems that revel in the joy of now, "bearing the *now*/ Along in its delicious ripeness, enough," even as the source of that joy has only a short time left to share it. As a dog lover, I admit the dog poems were my special request.

Moving from the theme of dog as best friend to the theme of human friendship, current Utah poet laureate, Lance Larsen, examines "This Slippery Servant Called Water," in a lyrical essay/prose poem hybrid form. Then he studies dreams told by kids at the YMCA, and one of the dreams involves a "thresher machine," which moves us into a memoir by Jack Remick about his grandfather's farm, with its themes of water and harvest, the value of prairie, the "epicenters of human life and dignity and hope."

If you get the feeling from these first four entries that the anthology is organized to let the writings play off each other and reflect common themes and insights, you've caught the spirit of it quite nicely. We wanted the book to follow a loosely woven thread, just as the readings do at our Helicon West events.

Remick's farming grandfather gives way to the "Mr. Fix-It" father in a William Trowbridge poem, after which Bill veers off into teen idols and B-movies, giving us a good belly-laugh before he brings it back down to a different perspective from Coles' beloved aging dogs, that of the old "bad dog" leaving its human family, "going to get lost, like a good dog."

Jennifer Sinor picks up the family thread and steeps it in the art and letters of O'Keefe. Yes, the memoir is written in 2000-something and the artist died in 1986, but that doesn't stop Sinor and her family from having an intimate relationship with O'Keefe. "She knocked on my door one morning in early May, perhaps having heard I'd been reading her letters, and handed me a wide-brimmed hat before entering the house." Sinor's skill with memoir paints us right into the life she's studied, draws us back to the plains, to water, into canyons and sky. Sinor is a historian of letters, words her tools.

After the somber concluding images of Sinor's prose, poet Kimberly Johnson takes language forward to a fare-thee-well, immersing us in the vocabulary of juxtaposition, a Hopkins-like glory where words can do anything. From here, the selections keep lifting and settling, floating and plunging, carrying their light.

In regard to carrying light, I need to mention the artists. Our cover art is titled "The Carrier." It was created by Mallory Culley, an undergraduate in the Utah State University art department. We chose the piece because, as we told Mallory, it embodies what Helicon West seems to be: a gathering of voices that is immediate, contemplative, and sometimes haunting, with a hint of past lives, of humor and mystery, an illumination of inspiration and experience. The cover and book design were crafted by Maria Williams, a USU English and graphic design graduate who creates the fliers for our Helicon West readings.

So we have art at Helicon West. We have poetry, fiction, nonfiction. We have recurring themes that echo and shadow each other, that build on each other. Family, land, water. Seasons, canyon, water. Marriage, fidelity, longevity. Ghosts, legends, tombstones. Work, love, desire. Art, objects, dreams. The resplendency and quirkiness of Nature. Lisa Roullard's "ripening hope of trees," Anne Shifrer's white robin feathers "poking out/ from the nest, like a champagne flute." The bright wings of a cardinal, and knowing "when to bring/ the blue hydrangeas in" (Nancy Takacs).

At Helicon West readings, refined elegance can easily reside with down-to-brass-tacks raucousness. No topic or language is off-limits. Our PR blurb is consistent: "Free, open to the public, and uncensored." We maintain that allegiance to authorial intent in this anthology. There's a story in verse from "the world's first dirty book" (Hardy). There are cars, those symbols of sex and power. (Check out the rides from Long, Timm, Potts, and Dethier.) There's a sizzling set of poems by Susan Pesti-Strobel on the endless cleavage in "that little black dress" and on the undressing of Billy Collins before taking him to bed. Pesti-Strobel has a knack for hilarious yet lyrical description that packs a wallop at the end, as good as any punchline. A side note: Two of her three sons, the Nyikos triplets, have poems in the collection. Different voices and flavor—you'll see what we mean.

Susan and her three boys were there for the first incarnation of Helicon West in 2005, when it was Writers Read Weekly. Michael Sowder gave it the name Helicon for the ancient Greek mountain range where the muses lived, and West for the place it resides, where it draws readers from all over the country. Michael's work is featured here. Another of our colleagues who has been with us from the beginning is poet Shanan Ballam. In this volume, we get a small sampling of her Little Red Riding Hood poems which speak from every angle, every character, every fear and hope the ancient yet currently relevant tale evokes.

Chadd VanZanten appeared early in our history; Tim Keller came in a few years later. Both fiction writers, they credit Helicon West for their individual successes in writing as well as in leading their local League of Utah Writers chapter to win top prizes every year in all genres. Chadd and Tim pitched the anthology idea which has now become a reality.

Another exciting development in the trajectory of Helicon West was the introduction of Utah State University creative writing contest winners and creative writing club members as featured readers. We have set aside a special section at the end of the anthology for slam poetry, a genre that attracts our biggest crowds. Darren Edwards, slam performance poet, heads up this section with a riff on privilege and a look through the kind of microscope that maps the blood of war.

If I had room, I would mention every one of the authors who read for us in the last ten years and who generously contributed work to this project. But I leave it to you, our listeners and readers, to delve in as if you've been waiting for them to take the microphone and give it their all. Thanks for your support.

—Star Coulbrooke

Dinty W. Moore

You Know Better

As implausible as this may seem, his name was Charlie Brown.

Back in the 1960s we would have called him retarded, or just slow, though I have no honest idea what made his intellect function well below his age. The kid was goofy, and we all knew it.

Charlie was new to the neighborhood. His family was poor.

Odd how in those days you could walk just a short way and suddenly, as if a line had been drawn from sidewalk to curb, the neighborhood would change in an instant. Our block on Ninth Street was middle class – the men had jobs, but not good ones. Around the corner the men had no jobs, or were disabled, or in the case of Charlie's family, there was a single mom, recently divorced, with three kids, in a two-bedroom flat.

Charlie, a doughy six-year-old in a tattered t-shirt, had one thing going for him, however: a radio, the size of a small suitcase, with a powerful antenna.

One day I offered him fifty cents for the radio, held the coins right under his chin, and he said, "Sure."

I earned extra money mowing an old couple's lawn and helping the paperboy on his route. I was eight. Charlie couldn't mow or fold papers, so he had probably never owned his own two quarters before. I have no idea what he planned to buy with them. Candy? RC Cola? Maybe he just liked the coins.

I knew the radio was worth more than fifty cents, but Charlie seemed happy, and I somehow convinced myself that all of this was just fine.

The next afternoon, I sat in the garage flipping past baseball broadcasts, picking up stations from faraway Detroit and Canada, when my mother walked in.

"Dinty, where'd you get that radio?"

It was a test. She already knew. The ladies on the block watched everything from their kitchen windows, and though it is a cliché, it is true that news traveled from back fence to back fence as the women hung out the laundry or tended to their rose bushes. Someone had seen. Or someone had talked to Charlie. It is unlikely Charlie's mother would have complained: she was too new, and kept to herself.

I fessed up, insisting that the bargain was fair, agreed to by all involved.

Mom shook her head, said "You know better," and marched me over to Charlie's front door.

We knocked. I handed the radio to Charlie's Mom.

The woman seemed embarrassed rather than grateful. She offered to reimburse my coins, but my mother said, "No, those are for Charlie."

Charlie stood a few feet back, an odd, twisted look on his face.

Not much was said on the walk home. Not much needed to be said.

I was out fifty cents, and that didn't bother me. But I felt like the worst person on the planet, a liar and a cheat. It was hard to swallow.

Katharine Coles

THE DOUBLE LEASH

Blizzard to lilac. Dandelion
to leaf. Endless
variation of seasons I note

in passing, smells
I cannot smell: rotting
gardens, feces, musk of cat.
                              These two

run in front of me, golden
shoulder to patchwork, heads
lifted or lowered into

scent, tongues lolling. Ears
damp with their own
spittle and each other's

tell me, tethered a pace behind,
their journey's epic: tipping
forward to the familiar or
stranger's distant yap; angling

to my breathing, whispered
praise, my slightest
suggestion.
              Ignored.
                        The shepherd
throws herself into

any whirring wheel, to herd
the neighbor's tractor mower or
the UPS truck's packets
home; pulling her back,

the golden's oblivious
ballast, instinct heading
always for the gutter's

deepest puddle, her own way
within the forked leash's
one-foot range. As we pass,

the clans set up
their barking, as if we
were news, gathering center

of a congenial warning
din—mine answer with
disturbances of pace, an extra pull
or lollop, grins thrown

slant-eyed over shoulders
until one hears a call
she can't ignore, surrenders

to baying's ferocious
joy moving
muscle and bone. Moving
storm, storm's eye: happy

universes whirl in their skins
as I do in mine. Unknowable,
their fate. Mediums between
foreign principalities, they're tied

to me, to each other, by my will,
by love; to that other realm
by song, and tooth, and blood.

A Confusion

Not even a decent pack. Just a pair,
though in small rooms they move to multiply.
A piebald dog. A dog with golden fur.
One who herds. One who gulps each fly
that buzzes her, cracking it in snap jaws.
Tonight, stretched out on oriental rugs,
a relaxation of dogs, dog tired; a doze
and snoring. Then absolution: a bliss of dogs,
a conflagration, a swarm, unspooled. Odd
dogs, chasing the invisible. Like me. A fool,

a blaze of dogs, a plight, an inspiration
of frenzied tongue and paw; two dogs in a pod,
mathematic. An education. Love's school
in wilderness, its muzzled exultation.

San Marco's Floors

                              Only years later
Will I remember to look down. Eyes not
Undazzled yet by golden ceilings
But half-accustomed, ready

To stray. And so, crossed
By centuries of boots, peacocks draggle tails
And blackbirds poise in windless branches
Imagined a sea away, re-imagined here

And here. Every little bird means something
If only to itself. How like me to forget
What holds me, to believe everything uplifting
Lives in the rafters. See here

A pair of crimson lions laid in stone, gazing upward,
Hopeful as my old dogs, to meet my eyes.

A Dog in Time

Saves nothing. Dips and dodges. Stays
Out all night. Walks akimbo. Snores
Through dog days on her porch. Digs her way
To heaven. Peters out again. Barks

Just so I can hear her, feels delight
Build itself to bursting in her chest.
Has a nose for nuance. Follows news
In passing's present tense with interest,

Tracking sources to their bitter ends.
May or may not follow me. Depends
On where I go. In her own good time
Arrives, waving plumage high. Smiles

To have found me where she is. *Well met,*
Her gallant heart. Shoots. Flies straight. Can't wait.

CLEO AT FOURTEEN

This morning, my old Aussie's full of joy
And her own compact presence. Spry at heart,
She leads me out, her arthritic canter
Sailing her up the usual path, aslant.

I am full of the past, memory
When she could outrun me every time.
She gambols when a van of dogs drives by
And breaks out, just for her, cacophony.

Against the long grasses she sweeps her sides
And plunges headlong down the shrubbery walk,
A tunnel smelling of deep green and magic.
Later, while I drink my second coffee

She lies on her air conditioning vent. *Oh, dog.*
In her sleep, she wags and wags and wags.

DOG DAYS

Then there are the questions of the body.
What holds it together? What falls
Apart? All of us are faltering, all
In our own ways going rough and shoddy:

My love's arthritic foot and knee; my back
Doubly ruptured, and I was only sitting down.
But these two—they don't think to complain.
They just keep their noses to the track,

Tracking delights of passage, every smell
Of every passerby bearing the *now*
Along in its delicious ripeness, enough.
Could it be enough for us? Leave well

Enough alone, I always say. He says
Every dog has her day every day.

Dog Years

When I'm home, she follows me floor to floor
Without complaint, lugging fifteen year-old bones,
Settling once she knows again where we are.
Now I'm gone, she lies by the front door

Watching through the glass for my car.
I have never seen this—but I know when
I open the door at last, she'll be there.
My husband recounts by satellite phone the hours

She lay there today, rising only to make sure
I hadn't sneaked back in while she was asleep
Or to watch him fill her bowl, then not eat.
Every minute you're gone feels like forever,

He says, his voice travelling all the way
To space and back before it reaches me.

Lance Larsen

THIS SLIPPERY SERVANT CALLED WATER

1
Mornings I hike where scallops once swam, Lake Bonneville before it receded. We all have favorite methods for drowning—this one is mine. What soundless depths in this arid air, what ghostly leviathan.

2
All water molecules are cousins, all vapor believes in reincarnation.

3
Each spring a furloughed cop named Hank checks our bridges for snags and jams. His flashlight belongs to the city. His scribbled numbers to engineers. His watery eyes to a face drowned centuries before he was born.

4
My friend relies on genealogy to pinpoint stretches of river he fishes. The Middle Fork of the Salmon. Henry's Fork of the Blacksmith's Fork, which feeds the Green in Flaming Gorge. In this way he marries the promiscuous waters and lets liaisons of wet rescue him from the land. The Stillwater Fork of the East Fork of the Bear.

5
Some boys pee off Dead Man's Bridge, others send twig boats down river. Both are acts of jealousy. River we say, meaning current we wish would carry us somewhere new. Water we say, meaning what we can touch but never possess.

6
Don't blame log jams for taking out bridges, but displaced water chewing at foundations in a rabid race to stand still downstream. Likewise, don't blame snow melt for flooding but the frozen ground it rushes over, like a freshman trying but failing to make room in his cranium for Emerson.

7
Peacock Pool, we say, recalling a drowned boy sixteen years back, or the skinny-dipping Santaquin sisters last August. No strutting birds sighted in decades. Still we call that naked drowning swirl Peacock Pool, as if any other name would dry it up.

8

A decent evening hatch leaves me finned and galled: sad for trout I have lifted on my lemony fork, sadder for those I've thrown back.

9

At the reservoir, I once climbed trestles on a dare and looked down. You best know which pools are deep enough. I counted backwards, like a patient going under the knife, then fell through stations of vertigo. The water did its part, pronouncing me coldly and greenly, a single splash, without pretending to know my name.

WHAT SCARES YOU

Wednesday afternoon at the YMCA

The girl lounging on the floor said, Rabbits—because their pink eyes glow like lasers. Rabbits are nada, said her friend. Try blood. We carry it around every day. Every day it tries to get out. The boy who wore flip flops even in winter described an apocalyptic Sunday when he woke up and his Xbox and three brothers were gone so he was forced to read a book. The boy without thumbs said, Once I dreamed I was a broken-legged deer being chased by a thresher machine, then I was the thresher machine chasing the deer. Twin one said, Eggs—the way they might hatch into dinosaurs. Her sister said, Me too, only baby scorpions. One girl wearing her brother's football jersey said, I'm afraid of getting my face burned off like that freaky mom who ends up loving the world anyway... Actually, forget her. What scares me most is my parents getting back together. The boy by the window took off his glasses. You know that sound the stars make, he said, when you go walking by the river, between a hiccup and a hum—I can't abide it. One girl braided and re-braided her friend's hair. I'm afraid of my school picture, she said, the one hanging above my Mom's bed when I still had baby teeth. The more bad stuff I do the more beautiful I look in the picture. Someday I will become so beautiful and bad I'll just disappear.

Jack Remick

Notes About My Grandfather

My grandfather was a silent man.

My mother says that he was a man with high passions and a temper, but I never saw him mad, not even the day I left the barn door open and a good milk cow foundered on the bran and had to be killed. He didn't say a word the day I panicked and left the spigot open on a fifty-gallon drum of motor oil that was stored on a wooden rack beside the machine shed. He didn't shout at me the day I threw rocks at the chickens and broke a fine laying hen's wing and she went from being a fat and prime layer to the last chicken in the pecking order and shortly thereafter died.

I couldn't figure it out. Not that I did these things deliberately. I didn't choose to break the hen's wing any more than I chose to pour the oil on the ground, it happened. I did it without thinking. I suppose my Grandfather knew that, and so he also knew I wouldn't do it again, and I didn't.

Now that I think about it, his philosophy must have been that shouting will not bring back the cow, it will not pour the oil back in the barrel, and it will not mend the chicken's wing, so why shout?

He must have been in his sixties at the time of the foundering of the cow and didn't have much longer to live though of course no one knew that. I do not know how he managed to father the Uncles and Aunts and be as silent as he was. I don't know if he ever said he was proud of his children or if he ever smoked a cigar when they were born.

My mother was the first of eight children, all born on the farm, and I was the second of five children, all born in the city. By the time I was old enough to remember him, my Grandfather was past fifty. It stood to reason: a young man could not produce Eight Children, the Uncles and Aunts.

And they were all silent.

The prairie around the town of Plains is flat. It is the essence of flatness there, and of silence. From up on the windmill, when the light was right, you could see across the prairie. It was the farthest I have ever seen. You climbed up the windmill and looked out and you were overwhelmed with how little there was to see.

Except land. And distance. There was a lot of distance.

And there was this death like silence, cut only by the whisper of the wind, the bark of the prairie dogs and the piercing call of the killdeer. The sound of the land before the plow.

My Grandfather took his silence from the prairie, inherited it, if that was possible, in a Lamarckian way.

He came to Plains in 1906 and brought my Grandmother Carrie with him. Together they made the farm, they made four daughters and they made four sons, the Aunts and Uncles, who made thirty two grandchildren, the Cousins.

The land was fertile, the line was rich. It was a good mix.

We all came to the farm at harvest time, a small army of 50 or so, some of us for only a few days, others for three weeks to cut the wheat, to plow the fields, and most of the time, my Grandfather never said much.

The farm had been through many changes before my first harvest. I remember the relics, antique equipment that in its disuse had become part of the landscape, like monuments to progress.

The steel wheeled tractor with huge iron lugs on it; the outdated plow with the wrong kind of disk; the old forge that once had been used to shoe horses.

Beside the machine shed, an ancient truck with a wooden cabin and no tires rusted in the heat and the cold and the rain and the snow—its engine long ago salvaged.

And abandoned, its usefulness gone, a seed drill that had planted thousands of acres of wheat, too, was being eaten by time. This was the living history, artifacts from a time which could still be remembered. Not the drill nor the tractor explained the mystery of my Grandfather's silence.

The Uncles, the sons and sons in law worked the wheat fields on the combines and tractors. Each morning, while they waited for the sun to burn the dew off the wheat, they serviced the equipment like soldiers preparing for battle. They greased gears and changed oil; they filled gas tanks and checked radiators. And then, in the hot sun, they cut the wheat, hauled it to the granaries, and baled the straw.

There are photographs of them. They were all very young, and there was my silent Grandfather, the Elder, on the tractor pulling a combine. In the photographs they wore straw hats, and long sleeved shirts. Around their throats, they wore large red bandanas which they pulled up over their noses and mouths when the combine was spewing out its chaff, and the dust grew so thick it rose up, a heavy cloud, the measure of their labor.

The Uncles wore goggles to keep the dust out of their eyes, and in the photographs, you see them, hats pulled down low, and they are covered with dust and dirt and wet with the sweat of their work.

From a distance, I could see the combine pulling alongside the grain truck to unload its store of wheat and in the silence, the sounds of the tractors faded and the whine of the combines grew faint and I could hear again the singing of the killdeer and the chirp of the prairie dogs.

But the Uncles? And my Grandfather? They rarely spoke. Their work said everything. They were doing important work. They were feeding the nation and the world. They knew what they had to do. There was no reason to talk about it.

At harvest, everyone worked. The Uncles did one thing, the Aunts another, and the Cousins, all of us who could, helped out. We gathered eggs, slopped hogs, fed the chickens. Sometimes the older ones hoed weeds in the garden.

Hoeing was an important job. It was easy for a city kid not to know a weed from a watermelon plant. We all did work that mattered there.

The older Cousins ran the separator that sluiced out gallons of fresh, white milk into huge stainless steel containers, and separated it from the yellowish fat that was churned into butter.

And on the days when they churned, the Cousins took turns at the wooden, hand churn that after a while, with the proper strokes and care, produced a large mound of yellow butter that glistened with drops of moisture on it, and which, when you piled it up on a dish had its own smell.

During the day, after chores, while the Uncles were out in the fields and the Aunts were fixing dinner, the Cousins had the farm to ourselves. Any house which had withstood eight children is going to have secrets in it, and there were fascinating secrets to be learned.

There was a Monopoly game that had been used so much the play money was worn through at the counting edges; the game had wooden and metal tokens--a little car with wheels that turned. Metal hotels and houses. We played Monopoly for hours upstairs with the worn-out money and the wooden and metal tokens.

And there were books. Zane Grey novels about the Wild West. Detective magazines full of lurid stories about murder and poisonings and bodies found on abandoned farm roads.

And one day, while we were playing hide and seek, a Cousin found a large wooden box under one of the beds and we opened it.

It contained a dozen swords and knives, bayonets and daggers. We looked at all of the weapons quietly, wondering what we had found and what we should say. If it hadn't been for the magazines about murder, our curiosity about the knives wouldn't have been so high. But for days, we were careful to stay away from the bed where the box was hidden, until finally, a Cousin, unable to stand it anymore, blurted out that we had found the box, and the Aunts and Uncles laughed.

The knives belonged to the Uncles. One of the Uncles had been in Germany during the War, and one of them had been in Japan after the Victory, and they had brought back souvenirs. The swords were Nazi swords with swastikas on them. There were German Army bayonets, and dress daggers that had writing on them, in German, that no one could read. The Japanese swords were long and curved and came in wooden scabbards that were carved and painted and looked like jewel cases.

And that was that. They were there, under the bed in a box and for years they stayed there. Every summer, we checked, but nothing had changed. No one ever took them out, they were never used. War was part of the farm, a memory that was a complete mystery to the Cousins.

At harvest, the big meal was at noon. It was called dinner. My Grandmother and the Aunts did the cooking. Every day they fixed a dinner of fried chicken or jackrabbit, mashed potatoes and gravy, fresh corn and peas, green salad and Jello with either cottage cheese or sliced carrots stirred into it.

Feeding all the family was not an easy chore. Every morning, it took hours to kill the chickens, to scald them, to pluck the feathers. It was hot work.

My Grandmother taught the Cousins how to kill chickens the quick and easy way. During the year, when all the family wasn't there, my Grandfather brought out his .22 lever action Winchester rifle and shot a chicken, usually in the head, in the eye to be exact. But at harvest time, one chicken wouldn't feed very many, and besides, if you shot one the others ran away, so my Grandmother built a chicken wire pen and each morning she cut eight birds from the flock and rounded them up in the pen. From eight chickens she got 16 drumsticks and 16 thighs, 16 wings, 8 breasts which cut in half gave 16 pieces of white meat, and 8 backs, plus gizzards and livers and necks. Eight chickens gave about ninety six pieces of meat, but there were thirty-two Cousins all of whom clamored for a drumstick. It wasn't possible to get thirty two legs from eight chickens. Slaughter wasn't a simple matter.

In the pen, my Grandmother gathered the chickens into a tight circle with the wire pressing against them and taking a chicken by the legs, stepped on its head pulling the head from the body. The headless chicken then flopped around, spilling its blood on the ground while my Grandmother moved to the next one until there were eight chickens flopping.

Then, after the slaughter, the carcasses were taken to the boiling cauldron where they were dipped in hot water and their feathers plucked.

There is a smell to hot, wet feathers, a smell that is unique and inimitable. And as the pin feathers are singed, the final step in the preparation, the air filled with the smell of scorched cuticle. We learned that life meant death, that if we ate, something had to die.

It was a lesson that was so much a part of living that it hardly seemed like a lesson at all, and it had nothing to do with the wonderful taste of fried chicken. Later, the chicken pieces, fried and stacked on platters, were passed around the tables and no one thought about the slaughtering pen.

The Cousins sat at card tables put up especially for us, and when we were through fighting and getting smacked for spitting food, while the Aunts did the dishes and cleaned up, my Grandfather and the Uncles retired to the front porch to sit looking out at the fields they had harvested.

The Uncles sat on chairs, feet on the latticed railing, some of them smoking, some just looking, and one or two talking in very quiet voices about the weather. My Grandfather would chew his tobacco, spitting the juice into a can, and looking with the others out across the plains.

Sometimes, on Sunday afternoons, when they took a break from the harvest, my Grandfather would play with us on a blanket under the sycamore trees in the front yard. He had a game called Indian Burn, which he played by twisting your arm between his hands until it erupted in a little band of roughened skin all the way around your arm like a bright red bracelet. It hurt, but never enough to make you cry. And then, there was Ancestors. He would say, you've got ancestors and garments on your back, and the little Cousins would say no they didn't and spin around trying to look at their own backs to see if they did, and pretty soon they were in tears, and their mothers would say it was all right, Grandpa was just teasing.

And if we were really lucky, and he had a few minutes, he pretended to pull our toes with his pliers, and we loved it. He had these little pliers that he kept in a pocket in his OshKosh. They weren't good for very much because they were so tiny. I think he kept them just for pulling our toes. He would hold one of us down and pull off our shoes while we screamed bloody murder and tried, not too hard to squirm away, because if you ran away, you lost your chance to have Grandpa pull your toes, and you lost your reward.

As soon as he finished pulling your toes with his pliers, he rumpled your hair and gave you a hug, and reached into a front pocket of his OshKosh overalls and pulled out a fifty cent piece and handed it to you.

In those days, a fifty cent piece was a lot of money. Most of us never got any money at all except from our Grandfather. If you got off the farm with less than a dollar, you felt slighted, and when you consider that there were thirty two Cousins, well, it could add up. Not all of us got our toes pulled all the time, especially after you were ten or so. By then you were big enough to do some work, and you weren't quite as cute as the littlest Cousins, and you knew what garments were and you knew for sure you had ancestors, so you could curl around the porch column or sit on the steps and listen and think about the day when you would be old enough to chew tobacco and spit it into a can.

Somehow, through all of this my Grandfather didn't talk.

Things happened, without anyone even mentioning a plan. That was the magic of being on the farm—things happened the way they were supposed to. Suddenly, we would all be outside, on that blanket under the sycamore trees, and Grandpa would be pulling our toes with his little pliers. No one ever said it had to happen, it just did.

Through my Grandfather, I was unique. Aside from the silence, which I still can't figure out, he had something no other Grandfather did—a large knot on the back of his head that made his hat tilt down at a sharp angle over his eyes.

The Cousins often sat around asking ourselves how our Grandfather got that knot and we wondered if we would get one too because he was our Grandfather. But no one dared ask him what it was. So this, the most obvious of things, that knot on my Grandfather's head, was a taboo topic. He was the only man I had ever seen or heard of with such a knot, and it fascinated me from the time I was four until the time he died.

On the days when we drove into Liberal, I sat in the back seat of the car and stared at the knot on his head and wondering how it got there and if it would get much bigger.

Later, I asked my mother about it, and she said it was a wens, and it was caused by a hair that keeps coiling around without coming through the pore. Over the years, it grew, but it wasn't a health hazard, so my Grandfather didn't bother to get it removed.

Every summer, at least once, as soon as the harvest was over, and the fields had been plowed, we took a trip to Lake Meade to go fishing.

I don't recall that my Grandfather ever announced we were going fishing, I don't know that he didn't. I think that at certain times of the year it was known that he was going to Lake Meade. One day, he'd get a can of wheat berries, pour boiling water into it and roll it into balls. When you cook wheat this way, the gluten comes out and it makes a wonderfully sticky goo that fish love. I guess that when he made his bait, everyone knew it was time.

We took the big Ford truck with a tarp on the rack bed, mattresses inside, and a tub full of ice and food and bait, and we spent the night at the Lake fishing, eating, and looking at the stars. Uncle Louis and Uncle Dan sometimes muttered to one another, and occasionally said something to Dad, as they called my Grandfather, and he would mutter back at them, and they would know what he meant, even if I couldn't understand it.

My Grandfather not only liked to fish, he was good at it and he was lucky. If I caught a small perch, he already had half a dozen. If I got a good hard bite from a catfish, he had landed a five pounder and gutted it and had it in the ice chest. There was never a time when I caught more fish than he did, never a time when my catch was heavier than his.

When he fished, he would set his line and sit on the ground, his hat pulled down over his eyes, and enjoy the sun. He liked the sun almost as much as he liked fishing, and he never got hot enough to take off his hat and wipe his brow.

At that time, before glass pack thermoses and plastic ice chests, my Grandfather carried water in a gallon jug wrapped in burlap. The jug usually had a cork in it, though sometimes there were screw caps, but mostly they got lost, so the cork, with a string through it to keep it from getting away, was the plug. When the jug was filled at the well, he always dipped it into the horse tank so the burlap was good and wet. The evaporation of the water out of the burlap kept the water cool.

One of the greatest joys in my life was to be on the tractor beside my Grandfather, plowing or pulling a combine, and have him reach down and get that jug with the burlap on it, and pull the cork out with his teeth and, holding the jug in the crook of his left arm, guzzle the cold water, first swishing it around in his mouth to get rid of the tobacco juice, then, with great heavings of his Adams apple, swill a cup of water while from the corners of his mouth the water trickled, just dampening the bib of his OshKosh.

Of course I tried to do it exactly the same way. I could taste the residue of his tobacco on the mouth of the jug. I tried to hold it in the crook of my left arm, but I usually had to give up and use both hands, and he kept driving the tractor and looking at me out of the corner of his eye and when I had finished, he corked the jug and set it beside his foot, against the fender of the tractor so that it was out of the way and couldn't get broken or knocked off.

Gradually, things got complicated for my family, and one year we moved so far away it wasn't possible to get back to the farm for the harvest. I'm sure that everything happened the same way it always had—the chickens got slaughtered, the fields harvested, the stubble plowed, the jug got wrapped in burlap, and the fish at Lake Meade got caught. For me, something was lost. After that, my summers were spent riding a bicycle on hot pavement, or going swimming with other kids and being afraid we'd get polio.

And then, one winter, my Grandfather went into the hospital for surgery, and died on the table.

Many years after his death, I got back to the farm. It had changed, of course. No one lived there. The land was rented out. All that was left was part of the house. They had sold the barn and moved it to another farm. The land where the barn had been under cultivation. Land had become too valuable to be taken up with buildings. But the water tank was still there, and the windmill was working, because water is too valuable to leave in the ground.

Life has a way, in these matters, of leaving nothing but a few memories. No one could tell from looking that that farm once had been crawling with grand-kids and dogs. I walked around the wreck of the front porch where we used to sit in silence. But there wasn't very much to see. I went to the water tank and turned the spigot, I was sure it was the same one my Grandfather used to fill those burlap-wrapped jugs, and I drank out of my hand.

And then, I looked up at the windmill, and I climbed to the top, to the little platform that went around it where you stand to service the windmill and repair the blades if they ever break. I turned and looked out at the prairie, spreading out forever. I could see Plains, and I was sure I could see all the way to Kismet and certainly to Sublette, and I knew that if I squinted I might see Liberal. The wind blew stiff against my face, and the crank chain clanked against the metal struts of the windmill.

I looked out across the plains, to the grain elevators jutting out of the flatness, and thought how those small, rhythmic eruptions were epicenters of human life and dignity and hope.

There's nothing on the land now, just the flat, silent, ancient prairie. The prairie dogs are still there, and the killdeer, but it isn't quite the way it was in 1906. America can never be the way it once was.

William Trowbridge

Mr Fix-It

Cursed by the broganed gods who govern tools,
my father turned Laocoön with power cords

and garden hoses, Blind Pew with drills
and hammers. Screws talked back, nails went

rubbery, saws turned piraña. He'd sweat,
fumble, curse his way through the gauntlet

of "Directions," jamming a half-inch bolt
in the hole for a quarter-inch dowel, joining Tab A

to Extension N, skipping the ambiguous
Step 5a. "God damn it," he'd declare

to the unresponsive skies; "lousy son of a bitch,"
he'd save for our electric mower, whose cord

he'd sever every other turn. A combat vet
with two Bronze Stars, he soldiered on

till the day he bought the canister of "Gro-Brite,"
advertised to turn your lawn "lush

as the greens at Pebble Beach." An I.E.D.
in his uncertain grip, it worked by pumping air

to force the liquid out the nozzle. He took
the contents in the face, the metal lid

grazing an ear. There was no talk at dinner,
only the A.C. chuckling under the window.

Proof of Intelligent Life

> "The four words that came to us from outer space
> . . . are: 'Send more Chuck Berry.'"
> SNL skit

In Go Johnny Go, '59, burgeoning
teen idol Johnny Melody is played by
burgeoning teen idol Jimmy Clanton,
fame now dead, though his molded

ducktail's got another 80 years.
Chuck Berry, who's just invented
rock 'n' roll and whose song provides
the movie's theme, plays Jimmy's fan,

consigned to spend most scenes nodding
and pointing from the wings during Jimmy's
Cloroxed ditties. Like Richie Valens,
singing his theft of Little Richard's

"Ooh! My Soul" called "Ooh! My Head,"
Chuck's allowed his blink of spotlight before
it's back to pimping for the white boy.
Looking relaxed at the back of the '50s bus,

could he know that, in our distant century,
the world will still be dancing to his chops,
and even if we all blow up, "Johnny B. Goode"
will head the galaxy's top ten.

Screaming B-Movie Victims

You can see them on dvd or TMC,
stampeded by the Blob, Godzilla,
the Giant Gila Monster, by Them

or the It from outer space
or beneath the sea. They sprint
down Main Street, glancing over

their shoulders, coattails flapping, skirts
flying up. A few stumble and sprawl
or stand there staring up in terror,

shot from the creature's viewpoint
as they're about to be pancaked
or devoured. It's hard not to laugh

at the way they ham it up, ditching
inhibitions for the primal shriek,
bugging their eyes and waving

their arms as their B-grade bit-part
fates unfold. You can buy a set of them
in plastic, thumb-tall figures

sold for their comic kitschiness,
something Eichmann thought
he saw through the peephole

at Auschwitz when the Zyklon pellets
dropped and the Jews shrieked
and waved their arms, made a human

pyramid up to the small air vent.
The bodies were laughingly called
figuren, meaning "puppets" or "dolls,"

which is what they looked like
when shoved into ovens or dumped
in graves long as football fields.

In a model made for Lanzmann's movie
Shoah, the dolls file to their "shower"
in Crematorium II, unwary

as the ants we used to roast by focusing
sunlight with a magnifying glass
as they soldiered towards their hole. We

laughed to watch them scatter
for their lives, then writhe and sizzle
like haywire windup toys. We were

Marines at Iwo, burning Japs,
who used Chinese as bayonet dummies
and were shown on posters as cartoon

bugs or monkeys. In Life we saw
the head of one, hood ornament
on a G.I. tank, toothless, withered

in the heat, mouth still gaping
in a scream, like some rubber prop
from Attack of the Crab Monsters.

OBEDIENCE

The ghost of it whimpered back last night
from a wet November fifty years ago:
a scraggly cocker that shadowed me home
from school and, when I let it in, ignored
a meal to snuffle crotches and hump legs
as if to win us with what it knew of love,
its sad pink dick unsheathed like a gut
protruding from a wound, its rheumy eyes
spinning with dread, its odor of mushroom
and shit making itself at home in our carpet.

"No. Bad dog. Down," we said, shoving it away
till my father got it in the car, and we drove off
through the dark to a cornfield outside town,
where the rain blew and it slumped off right away,
going to get lost, like a good dog.

Jennifer Sinor

HOLES IN THE SKY

I have been sitting in my study with Georgia O'Keeffe for the past few weeks. She knocked on my door one morning in early May, perhaps having heard I had been reading her letters, and handed me a wide-brimmed hat before entering the house. We've spent most of the last days sitting across from one another, her in an old armchair upholstered in mauve, me in a straight-backed chair with popped springs. As is her nature, she is quiet most of the time, preferring silence to talk, words only getting in the way. On the first day we sat together, the tulips in my front yard an army of color, she said, "Words have been misused."

In my confusion, I asked her if she meant a particular word, something I had said or not said.

She shook her head and continued, "The usual words don't express my meaning and I can't make up new ones for it."

I nodded, knowing all too well how language fails us. Paint, of course, is her syntax, pigment, her letters. "I paint," she once said, "because color is a significant language to me." In that medium, I am illiterate.

O'Keeffe prefers herbal tea, as do I, and we both like to sit in the morning silence, my young sons off at school, the house settling around us. Steam from the cups clings to our cheeks and chins. The heater glows at our feet, cutting a path of warmth along the floor of my basement study. As if around a campfire, we turn our legs, brown our calves. During the past three weeks, sitting under my one window, we have said little. In her worn face, crumpled like a sack, felted with use, I see my husband's Aunt Eileen who, at 96, is two years younger than O'Keeffe but who is dying in a bed in Richmond, Virginia, thousands of miles from here. "We are all dying," I said to Michael, my husband, when we first learned Eileen was no longer eating. "Yes," he said, "but Eileen is dying faster."

Our cat, Luna, pushes open the door to my study, her white paws bright against the dark carpet. "That's fine, fine," O'Keeffe says and pats the space next to her. Eileen uses the same phrase.

"That's fine," O'Keeffe repeats as Luna comes closer to her outstretched hand. At ninety-eight, sight failing, bones thinned to translucence, everything seems to be fine.

* * *

Before my first son, Aidan, was born, I drew a picture of the two of us running in the winter dark while the rest of the world slept. We appeared very small as we ran along the floor of Cache Valley, in northern Utah, the Bear Mountains rising in black like a quilt set to cover the earth for winter. My legs churned under me, bent at the knees, caught in that moment when neither foot has contact with the ground. I was flying, and my hair trailed out like a scarf.

I drew Aidan running as well, inside of me. He assumed the same pose in my belly, bent knees, churning legs, only he was swimming rather than flying, making his way through water as warm as the South Pacific, in darkness that even stars failed to pierce. While I listened for the approach of a car or the bark of a dog let loose on its morning business, I imagined he ran to the shush of waves, an ebb and flow of water that matched the rhythm of my stride.

* * *

I ask O'Keeffe about Eileen. "How long, do you think, before she dies?" A silly question. O'Keeffe has never met Eileen, only knows of her as the old woman whose body is failing, whose downward slide has Michael and me huddled during parts of the day trying to decide if and when he should fly back. She looks out the one window in my study, a basement window that frames the cherry tree in our backyard, and, beyond that, the sky.

From our position, underground, we are afforded the same perspective as her painting *The Lawrence Tree*, where the viewer looks up from beneath the tree into branches and stars. A tree standing on its head is how O'Keeffe described it to her friends. What I love about that work—as with so many of her paintings—is that our own place in space, as viewers, is uncertain. Are we on our backs on the ground? On a bench? In our graves? Or are we floating in space like one of her skulls, hovering in a kind of ecstasy?

The Lawrence tree exists. You can go to northern New Mexico, to the Lawrence Ranch, and sit underneath it. It is site specific like many of her landscapes. But when you look up into the tree, you won't see what O'Keeffe saw. Your tree won't be nearly as wondrous. That's because O'Keeffe faithfully rendered aspects of the actual landscape—the contours, the planes—and then abstracted them to get at the emotional truth of her vision. In *The Lawrence Tree* we have a record of what it meant for her to look up into those branches, the bliss she felt in its limbs.

I ponder the green leaves of the cherry tree outside the window of my study. Because O'Keeffe has not told me how to hold the death of Eileen in my hands, I ask her about the tree.

"What do you see?"

She sits in a chair beside me, Luna curled up in her lap. The house remains quiet except for the click of the space heater. O'Keeffe pets Luna, the long slender fingers made famous by Stieglitz running the length of the cat's body. I want to be the cat, to be petted by the hands that turned a tree on its head.

"Telephone wires."

* * *

Michael brings scrambled eggs and butter-soaked toast covered with raspberry jelly that streaks the plate like blood. My finger follows the sticky river, red to my lips and the taste of childhood. Minutes later he arrives with juice, careful not to spill, and sets the glass on the nightstand. The bedroom remains dark in midday as if someone in the house suffers a migraine or the stomach flu. The yellow eggs warm me from the inside out.

* * *

I was born in Texas, but it took O'Keeffe two decades before she made her way from her birthplace in Sun Prairie, Wisconsin, to the Lone Star State. When she did, it would feel like coming home. The boundless sky, the open plains.

She wrote to Stieglitz in 1916, two years before they became lovers, "The plains---the wonderful great big sky--makes me want to breathe so deep that I'll break--There is so much of it—I want to get outside of it all—I would if I could—even if it killed me—."

The open space of the plains would influence O'Keeffe throughout her career. You only have to look at her work to know that O'Keeffe was fascinated with holes, spaces. Empty places that pulse with energy. I am thinking of her pelvis bones, her flowers, her canyons. I read once that O'Keeffe had a "passion for voids" and that her use of frames—whether fishhooks, cattle bones, or geologic formations---are reminiscent of the open windows in nineteenth-century paintings, windows that created feelings of longing, provided thresholds into the unknown. The window frames the abyss, contains it long enough for us to see it, experience it. Like a sculpture, the window simultaneously shapes the emptiness and births it.

The holes in O'Keeffe's work, her voids, were the subject. Not the bone, but what can be seen through it. And what she saw was both beautiful and sad, terrifying and sublime, a space so complex, and charged, and personal, that words would never capture it.

* * *

Aidan plays in the other room, chattering a combination of vowels sopped in drool. Six months gone from my body, he still topples like a tree when placed on the floor without support. He waved to me from the car seat where Michael had hurriedly strapped him down, apparently unshaken by his mother's place in the snow bank. Ambulance lights flashed red across his face.

* * *

In her autobiography, O'Keeffe writes, "It is surprising to me to see how many people separate the objective from the abstract. Objective painting is not good painting unless it is good in the abstract sense. A hill or tree cannot make a good painting just because it is a hill or a tree. It is lines and colors put together so that they say something. For me, this is the very basis of painting. The abstraction is often the most definite form for the intangible thing in myself that I can only clarify in paint." I see this in O'Keeffe's work. Maybe because I have traveled to the places that O'Keeffe has painted and know the way she takes what is there and bends it. Consumes it. Digests it. Reinterprets it. I'm not sure of the right metaphor. The result, though, like her landscapes, contains no middle space. It has elements of the real and elements of the abstract—both the near and the faraway—and never sacrifices one for the other. She would see no need for choice.

* * *

"Is it too late?" I ask, close to an hour after neither of us has spoken. I don't know if I am asking about Eileen or about my own cloudy ways of seeing.

When I look to O'Keeffe for an answer, I see she has fallen asleep. Her hand rests on Luna, mid-stroke.

Last night Michael's mother, Kay, called us close to midnight. She and Eileen live together in an apartment not far from Michael's sister, Nancy, and her family.

"Eileen is dead," Kay cried. I could hear her easily, even though Michael held the phone to his ear. Her grief could not be contained by a mouthpiece.

"How do you know?" Michael asked, voice soft.

Kay had gone into Eileen's room to check on her, just as she did every night before bed. She had tried to rouse Eileen but couldn't, was convinced that she had died.

"I have lost my second mother, "Kay cried. I could imagine Kay on the couch in her living room, surrounded by the antiques she and her late husband had collected over the years, strong, solid desks and end tables, all polished until they shone like stars. I knew how her shoulders would shake quietly as she held the phone, the tiny gasps that would escape her lips. Not large sobs, but rather constrained sadness, gathered and collected in the same way she had led her life.

When Michael's father died, we stood in the hospital room, Walter still in his bed, his mouth frozen in a final gasp. Michael and I had come the day before, having flown over the roads between Indiana and North Carolina, not even taking time to pack. When we arrived, his father breathed in long gasps, sometimes going for minutes before taking in more air. Then, in the early morning, just as the sun was breaching the Appalachians, one of the pauses became permanent. In the wan light, Kay, Michael, Nancy, and I circled the bed, gathered around a center that was no longer there. It was there I first heard the controlled shattering of Kay's heart. The tiny breaths, pants almost, of grief.

"Call Nancy," Michael said to his mother, the phone held tightly to his ear. He looked at me with eyebrows raised, clearly unsure of what to do. "Ask her to come over."

Ten minutes later Nancy called us back. Eileen was only in a deep sleep. She was not dead, though Kay had tasted what it would feel like when she was alone.

* * *

It was January 6. Eight inches of snow had fallen by daylight. Large, wet flakes still swam through the sky, like a flock of fish caught in a current running parallel to the ground. When I left the house that morning, I was the first to mark the snow.

* * *

We are standing at the mouth of Green Canyon, about a mile from my house. O'Keeffe hadn't wanted to leave my study, but I convinced her that days like today—May afternoons where the sky is charged with blue and snow still caps the mountains surrounding this northern Utah valley—cannot pass unwitnessed. Of course, it takes little to encourage O'Keeffe to come outdoors. She loves the natural world, draws her inspiration from it, claimed in her later years that the country around her home in Ghost Ranch, in particular the Pedernal, a geologic formation that appears in so many of her paintings, had been given to her by God. If she painted it enough, he had told her, it would be hers. No, her hesitation this afternoon is not from her desire to be inside rather than out, but from her need for solitude. Translating the unknown into the known, framing the void, requires isolation. She wrote to Jean Toomer in 1934, "I feel more or less like a reed blown about by the winds of my habit—my affections—the things that I am –moving it seems—more and more toward aloneness—not because I wish it so but because there seems to be no other way." She doesn't like to be around people, especially strangers, and when electricity and indoor plumbing arrived in O'Keeffe country, bringing more and more neighbors, O'Keeffe almost left. At the mouth of Green Canyon, new housing projects grow like canker sores. I notice that we both keep our eyes trained on the canyon walls, the sky, the faraway places still free of "man's destruction."

We stand, in the middle of the day, in the middle of the week, in the middle of a canyon that was birthed millions of years ago by a river that now only runs in the spring. Juniper dot the valley walls, big tooth maple. It isn't northern New Mexico, but it's not too different from it. Above us, the sky.

"And what do you see here?" I ask, pointing to the scraped hills, the bonsai-ed juniper. "What would you paint?"

* * *

Last summer, when I sat with Eileen in her room, sun pouring through the window, the woods alive with birdsong, I knitted a scarf. Every now and then, while perched on the edge of her bed, ball of yarn unspooling in my lap, I reached for Eileen's hand and rubbed the thin skin, conscious of how often we restrict touch to only the infant and the infirm. With each passing hour, I purled the invisible flakes of her skin as well as the dust motes floating in the sun into a scarf I was knitting for my mother.

* * *

The snow crunches beneath my running shoes, January light thin and brittle. My breath is slow and quiet from years of running and my hair beats an even rhythm against my jacket. Five miles into my run, my mind is empty of thought, though my feet register the softness of the deep snow. I am running on cloud. And then I fall.

* * *

Marjane Satrapi's graphic memoir, *Persepolis*, tells the coming-of-age story of the author, a child growing up in post-revolution Iran. Late in the book, we come to a cell, the square frame in a comic, that is totally black. The cell recounts the moment when Satrapi returns to her street after a bombing and finds that her best friend has been buried under the rubble of her house. Only a bracelet remains. Satrapi's howl is rendered in blackness. Such emptiness is much more horrifying than any image Satrapi might have drawn, any words she might have conjured. We import our own demons into that black cell. We fill her void with our pain.

* * *

O'Keeffe was smart not to trust language. "Words and I –are not good friends," she wrote Stieglitz, just at the moment in her career when she first broke through in her painting. For two years she had been struggling in South Carolina to give birth to her own vision. When she moved to Canyon, Texas, the landscapes, the boundless sky, gave her the space to realize it. Her friend, Anita Pollitzer, took the charcoals she had been making to the famous Alfred Stieglitz to see what he might say. His response, though potentially more legend than fact: "At last a woman on paper." What he held were her early abstractions, sketches without narrative or figure. Two black lines—one fairly vertical and another lightning-shaped. A swirling ball of black. O'Keeffe had been reading and rereading Kandinsky's book *Concerning the Spiritual in Art.* Her work realized Kandinsky's commitment to emotional truth, the "departure of art from the objective world and the discovery of a new subject matter based only on the artist's inner need." Years later, long after she held her first pelvis bone to sky, she would quip, "Nothing is less real than realism."

* * *

O'Keeffe never lets others watch her paint, throws white sheets over her work when visitors arrive, so I guess I should not be surprised that she won't tell me now what she sees in the canyon walls around us. In fact, she isn't even looking up. She is looking down, at the rocks near her feet. She pulls a tiny white shell from the ground; it is round and swirling. I thought her skin white until she holds the shell. Now I see how many whites exist in the world.

"It's the shell of a mountain snail," I tell her. "But I like to pretend it's a seashell left over from when Lake Bonneville, a giant inland sea, covered this area. Thousands of years ago. We walk now on the shore left by the lake, the bench."

"Texas was like an ocean," she says. "Nothing but sky and prairie. More like the ocean than anything I have known." She turns the small shell in her fingers, bits of dirt sifting down.

"I grew up in Hawaii," I tell her. I know she has been to the islands three times. I have seen the twenty paintings she completed after her trip in 1939. I feel closest to Hawaii when I am in Utah, which makes people laugh, but it's true. Maybe it has to do with how you can see an entire train churn up the valley, the oceanic space. But sometimes I wonder if it's about the landscape itself, how beautiful it is. I pick up my own shell. "Such beauty demands conversation," I say, knowing, of course, that no noun embodies the emptiness in a shell.

"Do you know what art is to me?" she asks, her shell now in a pocket which she pats softly with her hand, "Filling a space in a beautiful way."

* * *

Here is a flower, she says, a black peony, and we see the artist herself.

* * *

I am shaking when I call my parents, the momentary warmth the eggs provided now gone, the cold having re-roosted in my core. "I'm okay," I begin and there is silence on the other end. "I was hit by a van this morning while running," I say, "but I'm fine. Michael made eggs. I'm fine."

* * *

O'Keeffe is walking back from the trailhead toward the parking lot, the canyon now behind us. Cache Valley spreads below us, rows of houses, trees, cars. I check my pockets as we walk, convinced I have left something behind. I realize, though, I took nothing with me.

We walk on the shore of a many-year-lost lake, between clavicles of the earth. The mouth of the canyon is behind us, and a red-tailed hawk circles overhead. Against the sun, he is but a shadow, errant comma in search of its sentence. Were I to paint the valley, I would paint the canvas blue, the blue of the Pacific Ocean, the blue of ancient Lake Bonneville, not a slope or rock in sight, the earth under water so that everything is sky.

* * *

When I turn, turn, turn—here, first, the moment before the turn, when all that aches is my head and my pride, sprawled in the middle of the road, snow seeping into my running tights, ice caught in the bands of both gloves—and then the actual moment I turn, just my head, to look behind, in the direction that I have come, because something tugs at my heart to do so, or at my gut, or maybe it's a voice I hear, quiet but insistent that tells me I do not have the road to myself, or maybe, yes, maybe it's the vibrations of the vehicle on snow-covered asphalt that I feel, hand to rail to check for trains, hand to doorknob to feel for flame, rattle climbing shin, then spine, then inner ear, so that I turn and see how thin the line is between here and there, safe and not, whole and broken.

A van the color of snow bears down on me, already so close I cannot see above the headlights—they are on, white and open in fright—and the tires, spinning black, the world reduced to grill and rubber and the sound of the future swerving out of control down the hill, sliding this way and that, weaving back and forth, tread throwing snow like fire, breath, the smell of rubber.

Like the animal that I am, I claw, four paws, toward the edge of the road, knowing I will not make it, thinking only that I must try and live for my son. I offer the van my flank in hopes of sparing my head, which means I am no longer facing the monster but trained on the pile of plowed snow that rises steeply like a canyon wall alit with morning sun. Aidan, then, is who I am thinking of when the van reaches me. He fills my body once again. Here, then, the van is hitting me. Scream of engine, flash of light, my son who cannot sit on his own without toppling like a tree, ice shards in my mittens, tire in my side, air aflame and filled with snow so that all is bright and burning. I am lifted into the air.

* * *

O'Keeffe and I are snorkeling to the Haliewa Trench. In a letter to William Howard Schubert in 1950, she wrote "I want to go to Hawaii again;" so we have gone. It wasn't hard to convince her. She sees the ocean in almost every open space, as do I. The Bear Mountains, where I live, is a reef without its sea. We could feel the salt water of Lake Bonneville lapping at our feet.

The mask and snorkel I keep in the garage fit her. We both wear child-sized masks, our faces thin and narrow. Even so, her mask is filled with water, the wrinkles like ravines channeling the water beneath the rubber edge. I show her how to clear it.

"Press the top of your mask and blow out," I say. We tread water, black fins windmilling our feet, and I demonstrate. "Do it in the water," I tell her. And we both sink back into the sea.

The Haliewa Trench is on the north shore of Oahu, just past Haliewa Town itself. In the winter, surf tournaments are held off shore, but now, in the late spring, the water is warm and calm. We are about twenty yards from the beach, both of us swimming easily. I listen to her breaths through her snorkel, checking to make sure she isn't panicked. Too often, beginning snorkelers scrunch their faces in fear and take deep drags of air. But O'Keeffe floats along the surface beside me, occasionally pointing at a colorful fish or dancing patch of seaweed. I don't have to look at her to know she is smiling. I have read too many of her letters.

The sun casts forests of light all around us as we head for the trench. Lying fifty yards from the beach, it runs for miles parallel to the shore. The sea floor is now only about ten or fifteen feet below us, but I can feel the temperature change on my belly. Goose bumps appear on my arms.

We swim between two worlds. Below me, fish dart here and there, giant fleets of bright yellow and blue tangs, silver tuna and grouper, tiny purple wrasses. The ocean clicks and chatters, simmers. Seaweed dances with the current. On my back, I can feel the sun and the wind of the other world, the one I inhabit, the one with air. My snorkel keeps me connected to that place. I hear the wind sing across the top of the tube.

If I wanted to, I could dive to the sandy floor below us, touch a head of coral or point to a particular fish. My ears would hurt with the change of pressure, and I wouldn't stay long before zipping back up to the surface, but I could, if necessary, still "touch." There is a kind of comfort in that knowledge, knowing that the "earth" is still within reach. But the deeper you travel into the ocean, the more you must give yourself over to the second world, the one filled with fish in neon colors, the one where the idea of ground no longer applies.

When the plankton arrive, we swim through rafts of cloud. I smile at the idea of water turned to sky, our bodies now birds, and watch the plankton filter through my water-wrinkled fingers.

Suddenly, the trench appears, as it always does, a canyon in the sea. My heart starts to race. I can hear my breathing increase in the hollow of my snorkel, a physical response to enormity. At one point we had been in twenty feet of water, and then, just like that, the earth falls away into blackness. The plankton turn to stars in the face of nothingness. We cannot see anything below us, in front of us, or, with a few more strokes, behind us. We are floating deep in space. Save for the rattling breath in my snorkel, sound has ceased. My eyes try to sort through the layers of black, distinguish between the black above and below. We are without degrees, an emptiness that is complete. When I look over to O'Keeffe, to the tiny oval of glass in front of her face, I see her eyes. They are the brightest things around.

Here, then, is the void. Saltwater enters the pores of my skin, tanging my lips. When O'Keeffe's arm briefly touches mine, the charge ignites my skin. What is outside, now in, returned to the saltiness of the womb. Black of crow wing. Black of night. We swim inside an O'Keeffe.

The part of me that defines who I am burrows under its wing.

And then I see the flash of O'Keeffe's arm as she swims past me, the palest of whites amid the black. The wake of her fins vibrates against my chest; tiny air bubbles cling to my bare skin and then pop. Her passage a comet-tail of froth. At the artist's movement, the emptiness is shaped, if only in the tunnel of her departure.

* * *

At the moment Eileen dies, Michael and I will be snorkeling on the Waianae coast of Oahu. We will be holding hands and following a green sea turtle whose shell is calligraphied with age. The turtle will drift in the current, poking the reef here and there, paddling his flippers. Sometimes he will change direction abruptly and swim right toward us, and we will have to use our fins to backpedal, the water turning to froth and lace. We won't know that Eileen has died, so our pace will be slow, happy to follow a turtle as he wanders along a reef of brilliant blues and yellows and greens. The sky will stretch above us, the sea, below, and someday I will try and translate the moment, this "inexplicable thing," into words, attempting, like O'Keeffe, "to understand maybe by trying to put it into form."

Notes

"Words have been misused," GOK to Derek Bok June 1973. *Georgia O'Keeffe: Art and Letters*, edited by Jack Cowart, Juan Hamilton, and Sarah Greenough, 270.

"The usual words," GOK to Derek Bok June1973. *Art and Letters*, 270.

"I paint because," How *Georgia Became O'Keeffe* by Karen Karbo, 117.

"The plains—the wonderful great big sky "GOK to AS, Sept 4, 1916.

"passion for voids," *Georgia O'Keeffe: Paintings of Hawaii* by Jennifer Saville, 45.

"It is surprising to me" *Georgia O'Keeffe* by Georgia O'Keeffe, unpaginated.

"I feel more or less like a reed" GOK to Jean Toomer, March 5, 1934, *Art and Letters*, 219.

"man's destruction," *Georgia O'Keeffe* by Georgia O'Keeffe, unpaginated.

"Words and I," GOK to AS Feb 1, 1916.

"The departure of art." Richard Stratton, Preface to Wassily Kandinsky's *Concerning the Spiritual in Art*, viii.

"Nothing is less real than realism." *Georgia O'Keeffe* by Georgia O'Keeffe, unpaginated.

"Texas was like an ocean." Paraphrase of a letter from GOK to AP, Sept 11, 1916, *Lovingly Georgia: The Complete Correspondence of Georgia O'Keeffe and Anita Pollitzer*, 183.

"Filling a space in a beautiful way," *Georgia O'Keeffe* by Georgia O'Keeffe, Viking, 1976, unpaginated.

"I want to go," GOK to William Howard Schubart, Oct 26, 1050, *Art and Letters*, 255

"inexplicable into form." *Georgia O'Keeffe* by Georgia O'Keeffe, unpaginated.

Kimberly Johnson

FARTHINGALE

Lo my pennyworth of windblown,
    hurricane
  of lash and whalebone,

how often have I fastened its billows
    about me
  sashed beneath furbelows.

Tight cinches the corset, tighter the stays,
    smooth and tight
  for the bodice's lacings,

but my underpinnings upgust
    from ankle
  to thigh to the untrussed

cyclonic eye of me. I'm the low-
    pressure system
  sinking the barometer,

the microburst havocking
    the weathercock,
  while I battened down to placid

seem, as a white-glove Sunday
    in June.
  Like all tempests I say

hallelujah for the cage,
    the isobars,
  the wickerwork and cartilage

within whose strictures wildness can wind
    itself up
  to the shape of its binding.

It's the lid sets the teakettle rocking
    at the boil,
  the shell's song the gunpowder sings.

FREEFALL

After the headlong
      theatrics
    of the jump—the propeller's hot wash

thumping like a heart
      in the ear,
    the hatch implacably open,

toetips pivoting over
      the last
    row of rivets to pitch into air! air!

fathoms of air!,
      the King Air
    plummeting upward from my body's absurd

downward majesty,
      arabesqued,
    my arms flaring turns in freefall—

after that flamboyant
      do not shrug off
    the parachute rip as ornament,

a flourished anti-
      climax. Look:
    the sudden nylon blooms

          like a poppy in the buttonhole of day.

        O hoped intercessor, beautiful groom,
        embrace this my breakable flesh
        and marry me quickly, quickly.

Star Coulbrooke

Harvest

On the kitchen counter
jars of pickles, dill with peppers,
peppers with vegetables
suspended in vinegar, sharp tang
masking (barely) the smell of cod
fillets broiled for dinner.
Husband is yearning
for longer life,
his cancer returning.

Wife lets him help
with canning.

He stirs fat peppers
snapping and smoking
in the pan, a slick of canola oil,
skins pierced, juice burning his eyes.

She cuts long strips of carrot,
red bell peppers. She peels onions,
he peels garlic.
They stand side-by-side, industrious
after dark, holding the news
inside, each thought a texture
of its own, the color of future.

Whose life will be set-aside first,
his, with its bright varied snap,
or hers, its vinegared spark?
Who's to say which will be preserved
and which will be tossed
like the skins and gratings
of all they've peeled-back,
brightest colors pressed into jars,
shelved, shining.

Sun Catcher

Glass panels gently tap
the window pane
in blue red yellow orange
fishing-lined together,
diamond shapes and beads
between.

They bounce
on gusts of wind
blown down
from snow-topped
mountains
east of town.

Brilliant crafter
who thought
to throw the sun
against an inner wall
as wind's relentless
mangle
sets its geometrics
tapping,
stops the death
of birds
who in their nesting season
try to fly inside
what's mirrored.

Now they veer instead,
no more crashing
into glass reflecting
what's outside, not in.

Sun catcher, hung to tap
the golden light and flash
its colors like an ambulance,
a therapy, colored glass
in a stiff breeze.

REPURPOSE

To retire on disability is to admit
the Stage 4 Cancer, so he gives away
his boy scout jamboree collection,
gives away his drywall tools, marbles,
clothes he'll never wear again—but not
his bandsaw and gouges, acrylics and brushes,
not the glass he finds in the garden,
broken bottles, shattered dishes
glinting in the soil, polished like the sea.

He plans next year's planting, builds
climbing-bean structures from cattle fencing
and metal stakes, tacks one-by-twos at the edges
where sharp points snag his shirtsleeves.
Glass and rocks and purslane strew
the ground where he pounds the posts.

He imagines a shop where his glass
will inlay the grips of walking sticks,
where his carvings will bring
exorbitant fees if he gives away
coffee (shade-grown, bird-friendly).

He'll have a ceramics guild, an art gallery,
a book shop. He'll crush glass in a contraption
he invents and make a million dollars.
He'll mix Italian sodas in his biker-bar.
In his Church of Blues, he'll play guitar,
serve greens from his garden, kaleidoscopes
placed at the tables turning his mosaics.

Sky's the Limit

Take the mountain range, times it by twenty
and you have the size of clouds, frothy white
whipped with gray, swirling, breaking off,
re-forming new shapes this first day of spring.

Along the greening roadside, sun
warms soil enough for sprouting new growth,
plants doubling their size daily,
hugging the ground, aspirating chlorophyll.

The air breathes pungent mud, damp spores
and rotted seeds wafting into windows.
Spring calls what's lain embedded and sluggish
so it surges on the waves of thaw,
releases stuck emotion, washes the senses
like dishsoap flushes aphids from curled leaves.

By summer, grief will be as dry and hollow
as June-grass waving in the passing traffic,
the dead riding in our minds, back-seat drivers
whose voices we question—how they know
which curve we should take, they who've deserted us
at the end of a desolate season, given us the wheel
and gone off satisfied into another luminous blue.

Shanan Ballam

GRANDMOTHER WAITING FOR RED RIDING HOOD: THE FOOTPRINT

Lupine's silver smatters
blue penstemon,
throats open, drinking bees.
In the shade, damp grass
flattened, the oval
of an animal body.

Once, washing walls, behind
the bookshelf I found
the faint footprint of a girl,
angled as if she were lying down,
gazing out the window
into thin rags of rain.

Tenderly, I cleansed her toes away.
I remember bathing
her small body in a steaming
basin, my cloth dripping
pale perfume.

It must be so lonely
to be the fading print,
the fragrant indentation
laced with musk.

I lie down so it can hold
me, this cradle
of long, fine grass.

WOLF WEARS RED RIDING HOOD'S CAPE

When the story is silent behind
its hard covers, Wolf slips

into the cape, becomes
a mind of clean wind.

His clumsy paws arrange
delicate shawls around

grandmother's shoulders.
Gently, he combs her thin hair.

A wonderful sadness washes
through him when he wanders

in fields glistening bluebells,
their heads bowed in reverence.

He hears their soft prayers.
For hours he labors with a paintbrush,

watercolors, paints sunsets for grandmother,
orange, purple, gold.

She fastens his pictures high on her walls.
He floats in a cold river,

opens his eyes under water, feels
the pure ecstasy of distortion.

He sleeps next to grandmother.
In the dark she tells him of baby Moses adrift

in his tiny ark.

Red Riding Hood and Her Mother: The City

Inside my mother's mind thrives
a glittering city. There my mother lives,
dressed in pearls and high red heels.
Sometimes her eyes shine and in them I see

a million glimmering windows, streets roaring
electric traffic, tall men with fat wallets
offering their arms, their delicious dark secrets.
And now I know she no longer needs me,

having lived so long in her lovely city.
I see the way she gazes out the window,
always startled and disappointed by my voice.
But I can hear a strange river rustling

under the house. At night, with the old shovel,
I dig around the foundation. Last night
I saw the water's dark blink. One more day
of digging and I can slip through the crack

and into the river, which seems to know
exactly where it's going. I will pack
a basket, build a raft, use my red cape
as a sail, let it slide me away.

Michael Sowder

Former Attorney Offers Prayer
of Thanksgiving for His New Job

—for Ford Swetnam

I thank you, God, for this poem today, whether or not it'll be any good,
and for a new home in a town called Preston with a desk under a window
    of sky and the cries of cranes,
for a full moon that rises over the Bear Mountains at twilight and falls past
    mountains at dawn,
for a river named Bear that tumbles out of a canyon, meanders by our house,
    with hot springs, kingfishers, osprey, and trout,
for our neighbor, Ezekiel, who comes to the door with cucumbers and carrots for
    the forgiveness of sins and hopes for our redemption,
for new words, like *jack-Mormon*—reminding that even in Zion apostates like
    dandelions grow,
and *gravity water* which runs down hills, which the city doesn't charge for, which
    rises over fields in silver jets, swords crossed against the desert sun,
for my commute across the bed of an ancient sea that one day, 14,000
    years ago, broke its dam and spilled north for hundreds of miles,
for the oranges and reds of autumn spilling down watersheds of Oxford,
    Bonneville, and Scout,
and the aspens that etch the fir-dark peaks in gold,
for light dawning clear as the Mediterranean,
while magpies rise from the nameless dead of the road where they dine in
    tuxedos—Republican cousins of the crows,
and for my arrival in Pocatello, where treeless hills fold over each other with a
    Renaissance love of the naked body,
a U.P. town of rails, cowboys and poets who, it has been said, actually—
    and I shit you not—like each other,
and for a boss who says, *Write poems, not briefs.*

For this is a beginning, and it's good to be beginning,
as Whitman and Merton and St. John of the Cross said,
for we'll always be beginners any day we're alive.

And now the streams are tumbling with syllables,
and the sea's rhythms are printed on the land,
cranes trace calligraphs across the evening sky,
and rocks break like words on the ground.

KELLEN IN MY LAP, EIGHT MONTHS OLD

In a circle of lamplight
I'm reading again *Zen Mind, Beginner's Mind.*

You play my fingers like piano keys, arranging
and rearranging them, finding

new patterns, melodies. You woke
wailing in the three o'clock dark

and we came out here
where you could play and I could work.

What is satori? Suzuki asks. *The bottom of a pail
broken through.* Coyote, mountain lion

walk the hills above our house, darkness
holding its wing above the valley. Orion

brightens January snow and the far fields
show a single yellow windowpane.

In our own ring of light, the joy you find
in my fingers a monk has no words to name.

LEARNING NAMES

All my life I heard him call her *Mother.*
Dad, can we camp out in the back yard?
Ask mother. Or, *Mother, can you
pick up the shirts at the cleaners?*

Now retired, they've left the city,
moved to a house overlooking a valley
in North Carolina. She tends tiny junipers,
rain trees, elms. He nails and glues maple and birch
for bird houses, toys, and hand-carved signs.
In town on Tuesday and Thursday
they teach farmers, mill workers,
to read and write.
But they, too, are learning names:

evening grosbeak,
honey locust, yellow trillium.

In the quiet before dawn,
I sit under a lamp by the window.
A visitor now. I hear them stirring
in the next room, talking in low voices.
Outside the window, slate-colored juncos
are chirping and flitting in rhododendron leaves,
and I hear him softly say,
Kathleen, the way he must
have said it, thirty years ago.

Aidan Looks at the Moon

After the bugling of elk
and dinner by the wood stove,
we turned in, slept until midnight,
when you woke crying.
I carried you out of the cabin,
across the porch, where September
poured over us,
with fragrance of sage
in Jackson Hole,
and you were hushed.

In the moon-lacquered dark
aspens quaked with owls,
and I looked at you
awake in my arms,
five-months old,
eyes like pearls
staring at the moon—
that lantern lighting
this field and continent—

your first time to see
the orb that lit the plains of Troy,
the face implored by Sappho and Sidney,
that Li Po leapt for, drunk
and drowning, crone of Whitman,
Hecate to Plath.
O Ariel, O huntress,

light this boy's nights
when he hikes these peaks
or comes home late from cards
or loving, illuminate his honey-moon
and housewarming,
and when he grows past
all my wanderings,
soften his sleepless nights,
as you have mine,

when I walk the house
in the dark
and find you in a window,
reminding me that outside
whatever carapace
of longing or fear
I've wrapped around myself,
something yet calls to me
from a home where the elk
steps into the river.

Maria Melendez Kelson

Starts a Family After the War

Of all the things he gave me— growl, prowl, patrol for control of our hallways,
furnace, windows, an MP's dark suspicion, and machismo's spit and boot-heel
for the female   itch and urge that I took after, as a teen— of these,
the greatest gift is trees.   Wash of coastal fog   sends green tones
one note lower—   valley oak grove in coast foothills,
Sunol Regional Wilderness.   I'm ten and hiking northern California's Flag Hill
                          with my dad who can't
stand keen-edged noise,   daily dish,
prescrip- or subscrip-.
Perched at the top of a tree upslope,   a golden eagle means   blessed
are we who share
        the strain of ascent: let's see how close we can get.

Bless Me, Pròxima

The nearly-wise, the next-to-best
came to live with us when I was six.
                Mother's widowed auntie, she got teased

by Father for swervy driving, her maroon
            Impala's dented hood sporting a silver
                        deer ornament dangling by one leg.

Because she carried golden ducats of Brach's butterscotch
            under fraying tissues in her purse,
                        I lurched into her hug

as she clomped an old Samsonite hardcase
            onto our porch. When she seized my forearms
                        like little brown twigs a witch might gather and burn,

the pulse of suburbia
            pressed its impossible promises
                        into my blood.

I saw, for the first time,
   our chartreuse garage door's
   peeling paint, the cement cracking

at the bottom of our empty fish pond,
   the evergreen shrub bursting with birds
     drunk on hard, red berries.

Branches and wings, twitching tails,
   needles, all screened our windows
     from the street, the whole paved catastrophe

reeling in a cantata of desperation,
under spells that failed and failed
   to keep cars from squishing cats,

and I slipped my hand
   into the gap beside the magnetic clasp
     of her sagging leather bag, clawed around

til I found the tell-tale prickle of twisted plastic
   and accepted Próxima into my family
   the way primer accepts paint.

Despite her muttering about curtains,
   her incessant conjuring of lawns from a brew
     of chicken shit & sprinklers,

she never had me hoodwinked;
   I somehow knew there were mountain lions
     prowling the hills around us.

My father, kind to her
   for keeping us close enough to safe,
     and decently dressed, never bought her religion:

robin, black ant, xmas card, mousetrap mumbo-jumbo.
   He hung pictures of languid African lions
   around the house, so I dreamed of big cats

batting away the screen door,
   rolling their nonchalant shoulders
   through our four-bedroom one-story,

not seeing me, exactly,
>> since I held my breath and didn't move—but I knew—
>> I'd seen the wildebeest calf on Wild Kingdom—

knew I was one sad bleat,
>> one baby stumble away
>> from a fatal pounce.

Stephen Tuttle

The Scold

1

She's standing there in the doorway, just standing there. And we have to wonder why she's standing there like that, like someone who sees a doorway not as a thing to pass through, but as a thing to stand in, making a point by not passing through, refusing to pass through. Why is she standing there in our doorway – it is ours – and not passing through and not going away and not saying more than she is saying? What does she want? Because she must want something? Standing there in the doorway like that must mean something.

2

She has asked us to please consider others, to be considerate of others who might be nearby, who might live on the other sides of these walls so thin they will hardly support a nail, these walls so thin they will hardly contain the heat we all pay too much for.

3

Are we inconsiderate people? Are ours the actions of people who fail to consider others? This look that passes between us, this look that hangs in the air like our frozen breath, this look says that we do not think we are the people she thinks we are. This looks says that one of us should say to the woman that we are not culprits if culprits are what she's after. This look is content to assume the passive voice and say that perhaps a mistake has been made.

4

The baby, she says, the baby. And we say, the baby? And she says that it would take so little, really, a little consideration is all she asks. All she asks, she says, standing there in the doorway that is very clearly ours and not hers is that perhaps we might consider others a bit more than we have. And here she raises up just a little, pushes forward onto the balls of her feet, stretches her neck like she's a bird. She leans through the doorway that is ours and not hers, peers into the space that is ours and not hers, looking for the baby, the baby, that sweet, sweet, inconsiderate baby.

5

We are not inconsiderate people. We are not, of course, unaware of these thin walls that will do so little to muffle sounds meant for other ears. And we have wished – haven't we – for walls just a bit thicker than these. But the baby? The baby is a baby. The baby has been a perfect baby, an ideal baby, a model baby. The baby has performed babiness with such perfection, such total perfection.

6

We have not slept well, it is true. And we have smiled our thin smiles and said to each other that one day, soon enough, we might refer back to this exhaustion like the others have done (have claimed to have done). And there have already been moments we regret, moments in which we have said oh, hell, or dammit, or when we sighed so heavily it was as though we had cursed our god or the graves of our grandmothers. There have been these moments – these moments that are ours, that belong to us and us alone – that are no business of this woman whose head, like a periscope, keeps searching for the inconsiderate baby.

7

We have not told her she can't come through the doorway. We have not told her she can. We opened the door, as considerate people would. We said hello and smiled, as considerate people do. We allowed our brows to wrinkle, our faces to assume expressions of consternation, as any considerate people must, when she said that there was something the matter, something in need of correction. Our heads bobbed up and down while she talked, in a continuous state of agreement. Our heads said everything there was to say: that we are considerate people who will listen to the pleas of a hunched, old woman, who will wait patiently through her senseless preamble, who will speak in hushed tones when hushed tones are appropriate.

8

But, the baby? The perfect baby? The sweet baby that is ours and not hers? There has been crying, certainly. Oh, how our sweet, perfect baby cries when crying is necessary, when crying is the perfect, sweet, appropriate thing for a baby to do. Oh, how our baby cries when a baby ought to cry, when a baby must cry, when a baby would be mistaken not to cry. All that crying, all that crying, oh sweet baby, the crying you can do. But it's part of the equation, isn't it? Isn't there an equation somewhere that always ends with crying, that must end with crying? Isn't crying at the end of that equation and others, too? Weren't we told to brace ourselves for this? Weren't we?

9

She cranes her neck, clearly dissatisfied. She allows her weight, the little there is of it, to fall back to where it belongs, on her side of the doorway, the side that is not ours, the side that is also not exactly hers. Her face has this thing about it, this fixity. Her face is so perfectly unchanging. Her eyes are wide open but seem so flat and sleepy. Her lips are thin and form a perfectly straight line that looks as though it has never smiled. Her face is perfect and awful. Her face is perfect and mean. Her face is ready, at any moment, to assume a scowl, to glower.

10

May I? she says, and uses her hands to make a motion that suggests she is giving us something. She turns her palms toward us and opens her arms as though to escort herself into the room. No, we say, no she may not. And that does the trick. That puts a little curve in her perfectly straight, perfectly flat, perfectly vile little mouth. And then we apologize, make our own gestures – palms to the chest as though clutching our own hearts – and say, the baby, the poor, sweet thing. The baby, we say, and we shake our heads and purse our lips and let our hands come together like an empty cup before us to show exactly how sorry we are. The baby, we say. Finally getting some sleep, we say. Thank the heavens, we say.

11

The baby, she says, we must consider the baby. The horizon of her mouth has found its equilibrium. Absolutely, we say. We can hardly tell you how happy we are that the baby is finally getting some sleep, we say. Yes, she says, we must consider the baby.

12

She is on the other side of the door, the side that is not ours. She is in the hallway. She is in the hallway that is not ours and not hers. She has every right to stand there in the hallway. She has every right. We thank her for nothing in particular. We whisper good night as though we just remembered to keep our voices very low, as though we have developed, of a sudden, some pressing need for stealth. We give the door a nudge, a quiet little nudge, and let it close gently, quietly, as though of its own accord.

Rob Carney

Seven Circles in *The Book of Sharks*

The cousin of a shark is a manta ray;
and the cousin of a manta ray, a hawk;

and the cousin of a hawk is lightning, the ocean reborn,
returned skyward and alive with storm;

and the cousin of storms is a waterfall;
and the cousin of falling is the wind;

and the cousin of wind is erosion
leaving rock, the bones of the mountains, scattered;

and the cousin of the mountains is a row of teeth,
and another, and another behind;

and those teeth are the cousin of the manta ray,
lightning, the wind . . .

•

In a story seldom remembered, sharks were ghosts
guarding the afterlife

since their rendered bodies had no skeletons,
just teeth.

The shock of that discovery
must have added new verses to songs

and widened the net of old omens,
but nobody knows. Those details

aren't the details that lasted.
Only this: The dead

step out of their bodies, walk down
to the sea, swim out to the horizon.

For some, the passage is easy—
a day, a night, a warm current there to guide them.

For others, the journey goes on and on—
if they killed a bear, or left a wolf's mate howling—

and the water is cold as a shark's eyes.
And then they see the fins.

•

Under the first full moon of summer,
they would carry bowls of water,

the light reflected on the surface making more,
a procession of moons moving forward.

In the center of town was a rowboat
being filled one bowl at a time,

and this was the boat of anyone lost at sea,
gone without a burial.

Those in mourning floated candles and petals.
There may have been music on flute or strings,

but we don't know; it's a ritual fallen away,
and all we have left are the wives' tales.

They say their empty bowls filled with quieter sorrow,
and with memories of the dead to carry home.

They say the boat would be gone come sunrise,
just the anchor there,

still as a headstone
by others from the years before.

•

We have one such anchor on display in the museum,
arrangements of fishhooks,

even spears tipped long ago with sharks' teeth,
and figure, *That's that*,

think the past
fits into our pockets.

We wander about
then buy a bar-code souvenir.

But the past is more like the wind behind us,
and the present more like a ship,

and the only pockets on a ship that matter
are the sails . . .

•

and they're wrong about the skeletons,
apart from the age of the bones,

bones buried deep but seated upright together,
all of them facing the sea—

so the ancient world believed in guardian spirits
watching over the living,

and a salmon was placed with the deceased
to keep the spirit fed.

Fish bones wrapped in deerskin
were discovered in every grave—

a plausible explanation, but it's wrong.
The living were playing the part of angels,

guiding the dead to the edge of heaven,
seating them upright to find Forever in the waves.

But what about the salmon?
Well, that's counterclockwise too:

The salmon were meant as an offering,
a present for the sharks,

a thank-you for taking our spirits
into their home.

•

Spearing a shark means seven days of work—
that long to do the rendering—

and all you get is a set of jaws and teeth,
some fragment to hang in a window

or look at over the fireplace
instead of at the fire.

I've heard there are monks somewhere
using human skulls as paperweights.

Not to keep old scrolls from rolling up,
or pages in place while they bind them,

but to bear in mind
we aren't the measure of Creation. Just a part.

•

The edge of the sea is a teacher—
so many bones:

all the shells and the sand dollars,
all the barnacles encrusted on the pier,

even wood—
it used to stand upright in forests—

even ash left behind in our fire pits
dug to keep warm, to boil water

and empty our crab pots . . .
even steam rising up like the spirit of rivers,

joining clouds that drift above our graveyards,
and higher still

the moon keeps sailing through its phases,
all of them the color of bone.

Chris Cokinos

YOU SEARCHED FOR: *ELEGY*, THEN FOR *ODE*

These are the things of the morning : liquid
pterodactyl, sunshine toxic, alveoli made hazy
with commutation. Inversions dull
the Wasatch like too much 3.2.
Coyotes edge woad. Sausage by semi, coffee
by Boeing, roofs newly shingled
glint fractures in a kestrel's eyes.
Indicative of transmission: bars and spinning
icons, tones that interrupt. On a derrick's lattice,
starlings perch in strange legations.
You've misplaced the seasons like car keys.
You watch a warm November on cruise.
Though something like fall scabs the ancient shoreline hills,
though resignation is unsurprise, the bones
of birds at the Great Salt Lake
are still hollow, steam still seeps
from a cheatgrass median, I-15's little Yellowstone.
Beyond the faceted spurs, past bedrock salient,
in Tintic quartzite canyon waters, a dipper plunges
in the dark, water rising round her head
in a cirque as silver as glaciers
hung above Lake Bonneville. Decisions
mob everyone to breathe. Filaments attenuate.
How many speeds in this account?
Stansbury woke one Sunday morning in 1849
and wrote: ... *the lake with is peaks ranges & islands*
lay before us ... in great & peculiar beauty.

Shari Zollinger

Sister of Icarus

Our father's will
led us to make the leap
from ground dweller to bird of paradise.
He taught us how to make wings.
How to collect exotic quill
from whooping cranes.
How to use hemp
to tie on the broad feathers, beeswax
to glue in the small ones.
I remember how he drilled
us on flight patterns.
Just stay clear of the sun, he'd say.
And how he'd send us searching
for the trail of a Phoenix up steep gray stone.
You told me Phoenix tears could heal.
Just like poems.
That was the summer
I glimpsed your inspired body
and knew you'd test your wings
for real.

The day of the flight
I thought of our father
who told you to stay moderate
who trusted you with wax things.
He did not know your lust for heights.
He did not know *you*, until you were up that high
the air like breath and the golden eye
of the sun pulling your mothwings.
You could no more fly away than
our father could fly toward. Like a kite
you would reach out and taste
that heat, like burnt caramel
on your tongue. The tickle of singed eyelashes.
The feel of the fire-eater swallowing
enough flame to melt the heart. It's why
I could not resent your tumble
down the atmosphere, the melting beeswax

the scattered feathers, the violent impact onto blue water.
Beyond the reach even of phoenix tears,
your blazing wings scorched bright.

TORSO OF ADELE

Erasure poem from Ranier Maria Rilke's "Archaic Torso of Apollo"
translated by Stephen Mitchell.

Shoulders and hips flared.
Wild thighs dazzling.
This torso cannot know eyes, head.
Yet there is no place it does not see you.
Translucent gaze.
Defaced center gleaming through itself.
Would a smile change this power?
Would it suffuse this otherwise glistening lamp?
This dark, brilliant ripening of stone stars.

TORSO OF VENUS

I carry you in my arms to the table
set you down lovingly
beautiful little torso

washed in from the sea
smooth like beachcombers glass
I carry you in my arms to the table

but you are not glass
and the waves had to heave you
heautiful little torso

to give you to me, you surprised me
dear fragment of one hundred sixty pounds
I carry you in my arms to the table

the exact weight of real flesh
I love you because of what's missing
beautiful little torso

and what remains
a *terrible power*
I carry you in my arms to the table
my beautiful little torso

Nathaniel Taggart

Our Love and Some Objects

After Andrew Marvick's *Through Summer Rooms*
The wilting kerosene light spills a patina
on your curled form.
I dream of lightning and there is never
enough light in the largest rooms.
Strung from urgency to make
things the way we want them
(What reason is there to be like we are?)
I dream of lightning flashes, burning. We take for granted
the dark forms shapeshifting, rituals
as we fold into sleep.
I dream of lightning flashes that burn you.
I dream of lightning flashes that burn your
shadow onto passing freight cars.
You are always in motion.

Urban Design: The City of Zion Plat

After Andrew Marvick's *And all the streets were changed—I couldn't find you*
Believe along with me that everything happens in straight lines
that our histories can't catch up to us   that we'll get ahead
of this and catch ourselves   our breath
we know the name of Zion and the next intersection and
the next   I need you to know that all new cities are
built atop the ruins of something *(I know if you'd heard my voice
it would have steadied you)**   sometimes settlers try and keep
failing   this was supposed to be the place   sometimes it won't
rain for months but this near-perfect grid can't lead me back to you

* Quote (bastardized) by Christopher Hitchens in interview with Salman Rushdie

We Dream and Believe the Rest to Be True

After Andrew Marvick's *I think I really tried—I couldn't hear you*
I don't know how long since you've gone but I've started
to notice this city is crumbling   a patchwork pieced from

something else—a long list of all else entirely
I used to think I heard your voice seep from the cracks in
the aqueduct   from the spaces of trenched earth that will
someday sit below our museum   I collect things   I'm always
collecting things   you can always find me here

Russ Beck

America's Caveat River

I grew up in a town that had a story for nearly every run-down property in its borders. Most buildings had at least one ghost floating around its fence line, but the really haunted estate—the one where, supposedly, my great-great uncle plastered babies into the walls, where it's said he threw his wife into the well, where the land itself swallows livestock and spits out bones, where you can still hear screams coiling up near the hackthorn bushes and willow trees—is just outside of town. Just far enough to escape the reach of the city lights, but not too far that you won't make it back by morning. The location, more than its history, is probably the reason for the stories. If there is no journey, there is no room for stories to germinate.

My friend, Dr. Lynne S. McNeil, is a folklorist. She told me that it's common for haunted things to happen in liminal spaces, in the places between places. So the haunted house on the edge of town makes sense. Just like it makes sense that most of the people who went to the haunted house were teenagers—not yet adults, but somehow not kids either. It's human to seek out nooks to create the things we fear, and the things we feel compelled to lie about. She also told me about the theory of ostention. People act out something of the legend to connect to the legend more. It's not enough just to go to the haunted house, but you have to throw stones in the well to see if the motion of something falling will waken the long murdered wife.

I now live near the geographic center of the Bear River drainage. I can walk to decent water from my house. But I hardly ever fish it. Mostly because the best fishing in Northern Utah is in Southern Idaho. Some of it is right on the border. There's something in the trip. It's more of an event even if the trip distance is increased by fifteen minutes. The Bear River travels nearly five-hundred miles, but its mouth and source are only separated by about 100 miles. It starts and ends in Utah, but crosses the borders of five states. It's the largest river in North America that doesn't flow to an ocean. It is known for its calm meanderings and its white-water kayak sections. It is America's caveat river. Almost as an homage to the river that always needs an explanation, I choose to travel to it. I choose to fish those tributaries that feed the river instead of the convenient pull-outs where the Bear threads the road. I like to follow the fish to where they spawn. I'm always looking for the less obvious place to fish because everyone knows the story goes that you have to work for the big fish. Fishing trips need time to steep both before and after fishing. Where, if you fish with others, they'll tell you how the fishing is going to be or was that day. Where, if you fish alone, you'll think about how the fishing will actually be or was that day. You'll compare it to other times at the same place and you'll remember both real and imaginary fish. If there isn't a space between fishing and not fishing to think and create, if you don't drive past water that looks fine in search of great water, the fishing won't be as good. I'll never be a guy who spends more time on the road consistently than in the river—but, I'll always give the fish and the river the respect of a drive.

Kate Kingston

Photo Journey

Dia de los Muertos, Oaxaca

I walk a field of tombstones,
step on broken marigolds,
stare into the eye of the skeleton,
witness my own marrow. I pause
at the tomb of a child, trace her name
in alabaster, climb the steps
of the basilica, photograph skulls
and snakes sculpted in sand.
I taste mescal, mole negro,
and grasshoppers charred to pearly
red. I dance with skeletons
and street dogs, catch my reflection
in the hull of a tuba. I soak
my bones in a cold water spring,
hike to a calcified waterfall,
listen to marimba, mariachi,
and the melodious wail of a Katrina
aching through the cemetery.
I watch eight photographers bend
over their lenses to give shape
to sorrow. I take photos
of the women, their faces like urns
holding years of ashes.

Motheresque

My children run to me
through fuchsia swamps,
their feet electric eels,
their smiles crimson
minnows, faces of canvas,
canned laughter, arms
full of garden radishes
and lost slippers. My children
run with apostrophes
in their hands, mono-syllables

in their heels. They run
with palms open, hair trampled
by wind. Pine snakes
side-wind through their sleeves.

My children run to me
followed by newborns, toddlers,
teenagers, a herd
of children stampeding
towards this hardwood root.
My children run to me,
their indigo arms spanning
prisms and apostasies.

GREED

I can't get enough of language written in sticks
and curlicues, founded on twenty-six non-refundable
letters, clicking and hissing, language infiltrated
with assonance, the float of vowels like an armada
drifting towards war, the stern canons of consonance
guarding the fortress with its plosives and fricatives,
can't get enough of language like fruit lining the shelves,
jars of syrupy juice and vinegar pickles, my language
full of saucy *ah*'s, short, shy and handsome *b*'s,
this language rooted in the tongue, blossoming
in the pen. Can't get enough of language, all chocolate
filled and trimmed with lacy cream, this bowl
of alphabet soup and home-made metaphors, the fricative
lisp of my teeth when I bite into a word with cherry
filling. I can't get enough of that buzz and tick,
that whoosh and bray. Can't get enough of its release
into air as it rises between lips and singes ears.
Can't get enough of the hum and purr, the grind
and grit, the cacophony of street noise bursting
at the seams. Language like a piñata stuffed with trinkets,
like a pillow stuffed with down, language
with its restless alphabet climbing up my throat,
language that I savor like herringbone between the lips,
like lace between the teeth, like corduroy on the tongue.

Natalie Young

February Can't Be Stopped

Refuse the sugar cookie. It blushes;
besieged with crimson sprinkles,
as though a Barbie might use it
for a pillow, a table, a giant pack
of birth control pills.
That lob of icing holds too much
in its flushed skin.

Yes, I dressed the dog in a deep pink
sweater vest. I'm not proud of it,
but she is. The knitted lines,
the v-neck—a hot contrast to her
short, cream fur. Not to mention
how nicely it photographs
with the leftover Christmas garland.

Here, take this envelope,
a swatch of fake velvet
glued to the outer fold. Take it;
rub it against your thumb. Take it
and know that despite its hues
of Pepto-Bismol, I adore you.

Oh, our shameless hearts.
Everything is red, pink, rubies,
darker pink, brighter red.

What the Lion Says Tonight

A sentence in and it's not a lion.
A lion has blooming power. A lion is worthy.

This speaking thing is a creature without ethics,
nimble and small, sewn into a coat of thin wires. It would be
the person on the bus who won't stop
staring, the one who gives

a loud eruption to air, fury to a TV screen.
The one who could use some deodorant.

What does the hyena say tonight?
Between incisor reveals and cackles, what does it shout?

Something about being
a pussy. Something undue,
the thickness of honey. A promise to give whomever whatever

with a sparkle, pointed yellow iris. Syllables
dedicated to an understanding
of gravediggers. The hammered socket of a word. Of course
the hyena actually swears,

doesn't think twice
about his commitment to rebellion. A carnivore with the goal
of an adam's apple—
pearl in the prey—

four easy letters nailed together
with precision   F : U : C : K

multiple times. Says the hyena
using my mouth tonight.

Hoarding Egg Shells

You called today
to tell me that the bulk store you frequent
will no longer carry Grape-Nuts.
I laugh, tell you *that's too bad*.

It's Tuesday night and you've been waiting
for this week for nearly three decades.
Not to call your daughter about cereal, but for empty
beds, clean floors.

You confirm that *it IS too bad*,
that Dad eats so many, you can't imagine
it's a lack of demand,
that you'd be willing to pay two more dollars.

Now you're wondering if I see any
will I pick up a box—no two—*they go so fast.*

You waited for it; anxious
about mold, unsealed preserves, dust,
breakfast foods. Five children worth of worries.

It's been a long time coming—all of this
leaving.

DIRTY YELLOW BLANKET

The reason she cuddles up   the unseemly   is: *comfortable*
a familiarity with   a nothing-new-here

Browned lint balls around the corners   of her mouth   her crotch
raw, bumpy from the blankie

She moves faster through folds   yellow fuzz under fingernails   other places
Saliva looking for the wooly strings   covered in tongue
not even the dog will lick   Wants   doesn't want   it   but it's here

She polishes with Desitin   dabs dry skin with dots of aloe
still cheeking the comfy   mucky sunshine   A heart beats quick
wanders   clumped fabric

ends up the same mangy   it began   palm sweaty
can't peel   the sticky corner   from her

Cat Dixon

Last Testament in Snow

Words translate to known
language with every freeze and thaw.
The typewriter's floe punches along
not slowed by greenery; these eskers
are inked letters one must know
to read time. The ice glares to
blind spots for one cannot read too much,
too soon. The jagged glitters
the deep cold and when shrugging
off to sleep, one may find a trap
between two walls formed by the melt,
the melt waited for all along.

The Illness

When you arrive, I know
you're sick—the deeper voice,
the pink under-eye rings, and I hold
my urge to lay you down on the couch,
bring you hot tea, climb on you
ignoring the coughs and vain attempts
to push me off, kiss your thin lips,
probe your mouth, and click teeth against
teeth, a toast to fidelity and longevity.
After all, I've never cared about germs,
the isolation of the sick.

Instead I'm waiting for
your eyes to fall from your head;
the giant moldy blue seeds
to rot and shrink away.

Siân Griffiths

The Most Natural Thing in the World

Dan Wallingford left the cut site hoping to clear his head. The yoader was down again and no more logs would move until Chip figured out what was wrong this time and fixed the incorrigible hunk. Dan snorted. "Incorrigible Hunk" should be painted on its backside, like the names on rich men's fishing yachts. He'd worked timber since he was in high school and, two years back, he'd thrown every dollar he could save or borrow into getting this company going. Christening the yoader might be his only chance to paint words on an over-priced piece of junk. Hell, he could take it to Bandon and send the damned thing into the ocean while he was at it. Might as well.

On top of everything else, last night Chris tried to dye his hair himself. Marie scrubbed all night, but the yellow counters were still a mess of speckle and smudge. She'd been bugging Dan to remodel for years, like they could afford that. Now, Marie was mad because he'd called the boy a retard, but how else was he supposed to react? The idiot didn't even use the plastic gloves that came in the box. Kid went to school this morning with dye all over his hands and forehead. So much for trying to look cool. Marie wanted to cut him some slack. *He's thirteen*, she said. *It's only natural.*

Dan unbuttoned his flannel, the day heating up. June was hotter than normal. Might hit eighty degrees, even up in the trees. Fucking yoader. Way things were, he might as well buy a mule. Buck and haul the old-fashioned way. It'd be a damned sight more efficient than what he was doing now, paying men to sit on their asses.

He ran his eyes over the Douglas and Grand fir around him, gauging their diameter and quality, trying to decide if there was enough here for the Bickford contract or if they better cut the BLM site to the west, but he couldn't seem to keep his mind on the job. Yesterday, *The Register-Guard* ran a story about a woman in Alabama, an elementary school principal, who was out running errands and decided to drop into work and pick up some papers. One thing led to another, the way they do at work. When she came out to her minivan some hours later, she realized she'd left her infant daughter sleeping in the car seat—on a day over ninety degrees and humid. Stupid bitch cooked her own child. That was what America had come to. People so busy earning a dollar, they forgot their children. Now Chris was up to God only knew what, and here Dan was, "working," even though the yoader wasn't.

He stopped and closed his eyes, letting his boots settle into the deep, damp loam of untouched land. Dan figured he was ten, fifteen miles from the nearest person. Even now, after two years eking a living from trees, he loved this isolation. The dense brush, the scramble of squirrel feet on pine bark, the foxgloves, the rhoddies, the Scottish broom, the heady-scented cedar. Oregon's backcountry was no namby pamby nature, nothing like Portland tree huggers wanted to believe in and "get back to," whatever that meant. It didn't invite you in or ask you to feel comfortable or refreshed. The forest was unforgiving and dangerous, kill or be killed, and Dan knew from his first Boy Scout camping trip through his last elk hunt that there wasn't another place on this planet he wanted to live his life than here, where the problems of man and machine were supposed to fade into so much nonsense, background pollution the coastal wind could carry away through the fir.

Chris could use a good dose of the woods. Instead, the kid sold his .22 for a handful of pot metal trolls, some video games, and a stack of "magic" playing cards. Nights, Chris and his friends sat around pretending to be elves and wizards in some dark basement, getting fat and pasty on orange soda and Fritos. Most of the guys in Dan's outfit were sons of loggers, born into the work. Used to be, Dan wanted better for Chris. Send the boy to college, live a safe, steady life, a life where you didn't have to worry about getting speared by a tree that fell wrong, a life where you were likely to have all your fingers at the end. Now he wasn't so sure. A little danger and real work would do the boy some good—provided Dan didn't go bankrupt first.

If he ever *did* get a mule, he would name her Greta. Dan could see her, tall and strong and sleek from good feed. She'd be grey with long, soft ears he could cup in his hand and stroke. He'd hang a bell from her neck to keep track of her, make sure she was well out of the path of the falling timber. He could almost feel the whisper of her warm nose against his palm as he fed her oats and sugar. Because unlike the damnable yoader, if you loved your mule, she loved you back.

Only, the woods weren't made for mules any more. A horse trailer on the logging roads? They'd be run off by the first semi running a load down. You had to make camp, like the old timers. Live the life. Which would be fine with him, but he doubted Marie or Chris wou—

The whistle that split his thought was nothing natural. Dan had heard trees moan and screech as they fell, but none was ever so shrill. No bird made a cry like that. No animal. The sound came from somewhere up by the logging road, a little down from where he'd parked his truck. Dan tripped on a root as he moved up the hill, chunking his toes against the steel cap of his boot and falling to his hands and knees. His eyes traced the root to its leaves. Poison oak—and his hands had fallen in the thick of it. He cursed and pulled himself up, scrambling his way to the source of the whistle. He was an old bear, only bears were more agile. At Chris's age, he moved through the woods more easily, running over the tops of fallen logs, jumping down banks knowing he'd land on his feet.

With the thick tree litter, it was impossible to tell where solid ground was. Over and over, he put his boot in a promising pile of leaves only to have it break through into an ankle-bending pit. He could see the logging road ahead of him, the daylight behind the Aspen that lined it. Someone, a woman, shouted something, but the thick wood muffled her words. He lunged and pushed his way up, his breath coming in gasps, his pulse pounding in his ears.

Two people were on the road. Good. Another man had come to help the woman who'd fallen. Sure, Dan would've liked to be the hero for once, especially the way Marie looked at him these days when she sat down to settle the bills, but as long as the woman was all right, that was the important thing. Unlike Dan, the young man on the road looked like a hero, tall and fit. He leaned towards the fallen woman, his hair thick and brown and shining in the streak of sunlight that fell on the road. His jeans seemed to be falling down around him, like they wore them now, ass cheeks exposed to the world. Other than that, the kid was every bit of him a man to save the day.

But then Dan saw the woman's muddy running shorts pushed down and the fresh red welts on her thighs. He saw the earth turned inside out below her twisting legs. He saw the terror on her face and her shoes kicking out and the way the kid had her hands smashed hard together in his grasp. Only then did Dan realize that what he was seeing was rape.

"Hey!" he yelled, his legs suddenly working again. His foreign voice echoed off the trees, raspy as a dull saw. "Hey," he yelled again, having no other words for this.

The younger man turned. He was too good-looking to be a rapist, Dan thought. Slim, dark-haired—the kind of guy he'd hoped Chris would be. Guy like that should be able to get a girlfriend. Or maybe this was his girlfriend? Maybe these were the kind of people who had sex in public, maybe this—the whistle, the woods—was all some game for them?

The woman tore her hands out of the guy's grip, and he broke into a run, pulling his jeans closed and tearing away down the road, athletic in his striped running shoes. The kid could have been a wide receiver, built like he was. He should have had girls crawling all over him. He moved easily, the way Dan had always wanted to back when he was in high school, not making the team. This didn't make any sense.

Dan turned to the woman on the road. She hadn't moved. She just sat there in the ferns, staring at Dan and ignoring the dirt that clung to her running shorts, the hem now torn and hanging open like a mouth. Her eyes on him were deeply unsettling, dry and direct. Her lips pressed thin.

She didn't really have the legs for shorts any more. They were toned enough, he guessed, but too pale, too splotchy. They had that kind of cottage cheese look to them that women's thighs got with age. Her hair was frizzy, but she'd pulled it back into a ponytail so that it looked as if she had a mushroom cloud sprouting from her head. The woman was his own age, which made him pause. Why would that handsome young buck want to force himself on her?

She had the flattest chest he'd ever seen on a woman, flat as a ten-year-old boy, and her shirt had a Spotted Owl on the front. She was one of them, then. A hippie. One of those women who came out to the woods to run because they thought it was *peaceful*. Well, he thought, guess she learned otherwise today. He tried to imagine Marie out here on this road, running, but he couldn't. Marie had put on sixty pounds at least since she took on that job working dispatch. Still, the thought of Marie out here, of someone like Marie out here, getting attacked by some pervert? The idea of it threatened to choke him. Marie and some young kid who had no cause to be attacking women? And if the yoader hadn't broke, if Dan hadn't happened along?

"You all right?" he asked.

She narrowed her eyes and cocked her head, as if he was something strange and unfathomable. Or perhaps it was his question. As if, of all the questions he might have asked, he chose the most inappropriate.

He wanted to say "I'm just a man, nothing to be scared of" but then, he reckoned after the last five minutes, *man* must have a different meaning. He had a chance to help here. Dan didn't want to blow that. He leaned over the woman, but she flinched away from him. "Your whistle," he said, wishing his voice to be gentler than it was. "I was just getting your whistle for you. Here it is." He lifted her hand from the dirt and laid the bit of orange plastic in her palm. Her hand was cold, though her chest was hot with sweat. Still, that small, damp hand felt electric in his own. He found himself buzzing with its energy. In another time, he could have brought it to his lips, been a gentleman. "Let me help you up."

The hands he touched to hers were covered with Poison Oak—she'd have it on her own hands now. He wasn't thinking right. He should never have touched her. Why was he so suddenly turned on? By the way it felt to have her eyes on him? By the feel of her hand in his? She wasn't his type. Spotted Owl business aside, he was a breast man. Always had been. Marie's generous chest had been the reason he'd first talked to her back in high school, and even during these past two years as he failed her over and over, even when she started working again, getting that job, a job she claimed to like but that obviously made her tired, Marie still offered her beautiful breasts to him each night just the same as she had when they were sixteen and they parked her father's Buick on some long-forgotten logging road.

The woman unbelted a small, canvas bag from her hip. She looked within, sighed, and poured its contents onto the ground in front of her. Wild mushrooms, only, there was no eating them now, crushed as they were. She was shaking, and he saw the start of tears in her eyes, though she wouldn't acknowledge them even by so much as dashing them away with the back of her hand. "Shit," was all she said.

"Hey," he said. "Hey now." He knelt before her, reaching again for her hands as if his touch might be comforting. If this were one of those fantasy novels Chris read, Dan would be laying his sword in front of her, offering his eternal service. And he would've, too. He'd have happily been the hero. Maybe less for her than because how good it was to feel the way he did now: useful, doing right in the world.

A tick crawled across her breastbone, moving upward towards her hair. He watched it move over her throat, its legs tickling her skin. Why didn't she feel that? Why didn't she flick it into the woods? This tiny little thing on her jugular, traveling to her jaw. He could press his lips there and suck it away. He would feel for it with his tongue, find the little smooth button of it, crush it in his teeth, spit it out or, hell, swallow it because once he put his lips there against her throat, he wasn't sure he could remove them. He'd be like a tick himself—pull him and he might snap off at the neck, leaving his head attached to her as if it were the most natural thing in the world, which it was, he supposed, since ticks were about as natural as you could get.

She took his hand and pulled herself up, and he realized he'd been staring far too long. "I'm sorry," Dan said. "There's a tick." He gestured to his own throat rather than hers. He touched the corresponding spot and found his pulse hot and racing under his fingertips.

He'd expected her to react as Marie would've, yelling "Oh God," and grabbing at her neck. She'd find the tick and throw it from her, washing at her hands long after it was gone, one wringing the other, like in that song Chris used to sing when he was little, the one about smashing up a baby bumble bee. He remembered the way Chris had lisped the refrain, "Ouch, it stung me." Three years old and such a stout little fellow. Couldn't barely say his own name, the r and the s always tripping him up. Cut Dan right to the quick.

This woman let the tick crawl over the backs of her fingers for a moment, watching it closely. "Look at its shell," she said. "Its pattern of speckles? Beautiful."

Dan stared. "You know those things carry disease."

"There are worse diseases than anything this guy carries."

"You ever seen anyone with Lyme's disease?"

The woman turned her eyes on Dan. "Mr. Expert, huh? Well, I survived chemo, so I very much doubt anything this guy might carry would compare. Besides, this is too big to be a deer tick, and I'd be very surprised if it bit my fingers." She paused, flicking it off into the woods. "They like to crawl higher. Get into the hair."

Dan stood there, trying to understand this strange woman. If Marie were out here—if some punk kid followed her out here—but then, Marie wouldn't be out here. It was dangerous. "You shouldn't be in the woods alone," Dan said.

"If I'd been *alone*, there wouldn't have been any danger."

"I wasn't supposed to be here today. Think of that."

"I'd prefer not to think about that."

"It's not exactly something you can ignore."

She lashed his tone back at him. "You're going to tell me how to deal with what just happened? You have some great experience with this?"

"I'm not saying that." Her sudden ferocity irritated him. "I'm not the bad guy. I want to help."

"I'm sorry," she said. "I'm not myself. I haven't been. I'm behaving badly."

There it was again, this desire for her. Was it her anger, or her vulnerability after the anger was spent? He wanted to fold this breastless woman in his arms and protect her, though he couldn't imagine her allowing it, and that thing in her that fought against him and disallowed his protection, that made him want to hold her even more.

What kind of a sick fuck thought like that? He was no better than that damned pervert, running around the woods with a boner in his shorts, using it like a perverse divining rod that sniffed out women rather than water. The same engine drove both of him and the kid, only he could control it, Dan told himself. He didn't go around raping women.

The woman sighed. "No one's ever out here. That's why I come."

"Hmphf." The snort came out derisive, even in his own ears. What he'd meant, though, was *that's right*. He meant, *I agree*. This woman who would let a tick run over her hand? She knew where the dangers were and where they weren't as likely. The forest was dangerous, but the danger was what made him commit his whole life to them. The woods were a risk. Loving them came with a cost. She understood, like him, that danger was what made the woods both terrible and irresistible. She seemed a part of all that, as terrible and irresistible as the forest she loved. She was the one Dan was like, not the pervert. They were the same inside. The young man was what was unnatural here. Out of place. He was the danger they'd, neither of them, calculated.

The woman looked out through the trees at something Dan couldn't see and wouldn't see even if he were to stand in that spot and look through her eyes. No, none of them were the same at all: not him, the woman, or the kid.

Dan said, "You come out here because it's peaceful, huh? A place to get away?"

She didn't answer at first. Her jaw seemed locked against any word she had inside. It quivered suddenly and softened. She said, "You know, they say that the worst part of treatment is the drugs, how sick they make you. And it's awful. Truly beyond what you can imagine. But that wasn't the worst part—not for me anyway. The worst part was going in every week, and having these doctors and nurses look at me like I was just some thing, some med school test they needed to pass. They'd look at my charts and forget to look at me. Like I wasn't a human any more, just some big tumor, some sexless thing that needed to be cured."

"Why are you telling me this?"

"Because the fucked up part is that I'm standing here wondering if I should be *grateful* to that shithead."

"Grateful?"

"At least he wasn't thinking about the cancer."

Dan had no idea what to say. Her words hit him in the chest like a spade, her foot shoving it deeper, opening him up but emptying him as well.

She turned her fierce eyes on Dan. "How much shit is one person supposed to take?"

"I," Dan started, but he had no words to follow it.

"I should get moving," the woman said.

"I can drive you," he said. "You'll want to report that guy to the police." Already, he could hear Marie's voice calling the cars out, sending out police to track the kid.

But the woman shook her head and swallowed. "No."

"No?"

"No." She was firm. "All I need is to be left alone." He watched the lump travel down her slender throat, and again he felt his lips being drawn there, like that was the natural order of things. He couldn't remember the last time he had wanted a woman so badly. They could get in the truck. Right now. Leave the broken equipment and unresolved contracts and metal trolls and stained bathroom counters and every other worry behind them. Find a little hotel somewhere, some place looking out over the ocean where they could watch the egrets sitting in the pine trees like small white fruits.

She said, "I've taken up enough of your time."

"I," he said again, then stopped. He was going to say, "I want to kiss you"— those words, from a married man with a family to a woman who'd nearly been raped. And yet, looking at her, all he wanted in the world was to wrap his arms around her and smooth her frizzled hair and kiss his way from her forehead to the breastbone where he'd first spotted the tick. "That guy," he said instead, "did you know him?"

She looked away and shook her head, her lips pursed, her expression unreadable. He lifted his hand and brushed away a strand of hair that attached itself to her lip. The woman was looking at him strangely. He'd been staring at those lips, he realized. So full, so soft.

She backed away from him like she knew what he was thinking, like her instincts heard his instincts and told her *run*.

"I won't hurt you," he said, and immediately wanted the words back. Honest as they were, the softness of his tone had only made them creepy.

"No," she said, "you won't." She tightened the canvas bag at her waist, but her feet were still carrying her away.

Dan bit his lower lip. That young guy, he had to know her. What else would've brought him out here? But then, Dan wasn't supposed to be here either. Maybe it was all just some cosmic coincidence, some grand joke. Or maybe it was the way things were meant to be. "I have a cell phone in my truck," he said. "If you just want to wait a moment, I can drive it down here."

She turned but did not pause. "I'm sorry," she said. She broke into a jog. She said something else he didn't hear, couldn't hear over the distance that was growing and the sound of her feet crunching the dry needles as her stride lengthened. She was running the way her attacker had gone. Dan felt he should stop her, make her take a ride, but he couldn't see how. She was a grown woman, a woman who survived the worst things, the things he dreaded, things far beyond failure sons and a failing business. Short of grabbing her bodily and carrying her off, what could he do?

He stood there, wringing his sweat-blackened cap in his hands, watching her go. He needed to get back to the truck, call the boys, see how things were coming, get back to work if he could. They would cut the BLM trees for Bickford; this site was all wrong. The trees had seen too much. He didn't know what to make of any of this, but he couldn't save anyone standing around here, let alone his company.

Survival of the fittest, he told himself. That woman? She was a survivor. But it bothered him, the man out there, all he couldn't do or save. He had no right to love her, this woman he'd just met, but what else could explain the ache he felt as she ran away?

Harald Wyndham

East of Missoula

Wraiths of mist
rise off the Clark Fork
east of Missoula,
the sky brightening
so that the aspens appear
dark gold witnesses
beside the river
and small farmhouses
at the mouths of steep canyons,
the kitchen lights already on
as people begin their day.

What a country this is.

What a damned beautiful country this is.

One Last Voyage Round the Horn

For Ken Brewer, who loved the O'Brien books

The brave stout ships of the line in Nelson's day,
When they had their belly full of iron and shot
And their knees broken so oakum caulking couldn't
Keep water out when winds blew sideways in heavy seas,
And the pumps were manned on every watch and
They couldn't run against the wind as years before,
But griped and wallowed loose in stays like tarts –
They still had their hearts of oak and firepower to fight
Belly to belly and foretops locked with that old enemy,
Giving broadside for broadside and ball for deadly ball,
Until, with flags still flying mid heavy smoke and fire
They swirled down together and sank below it all.

That's why we love to read of their brave men.
That's why we smile, to see ourselves in them.

Lisa Roullard

CANTEEN
—for my father

I filled it from moss-edged streams.
Was taught
to catch the cold and clear
from the rushing,
to fill the curved metal body
then my own
and after to secure the black screw-on lid
while swiveling free the chain.

When I didn't blaze the trail—braided
spark—I followed my Dad,
never losing track of his backpack's
pocket straps: not the stream's rhythm,
this soft canvas tapping, but that
of footsteps. Pace. The way
he gave himself to the trail, expected.
Arc after arc of fern.

In the pack jostled
whatever we might need: bandaids,
Red Vines, a finger-sized cylinder
of waterproof matches, Granny Smiths
and ham sandwiches,
a Nikon in a leather case,
one spare roll of film,
two canteens.

To me, all this was the way
most things should
matter: self-propelled, self-sufficient,
but not alone.
We'd rest on the stillness
of rocks, one of us untying
the pack's hand-worn cord,
then pulling out
the canteens: scarred
but solid like my Dad.

When I held mine—it used to be his—
I thought of his hands
with their scatter of moon-like scars,
wear that went on
long before I caught
my soft reflection in its silver
curve.   So far, my hands wore
his radiant map of veins.
Pine needles celebrated
our boots. The air
tasted evergreen.

The Mailman and the Pear Tree

He'd realized only tree,
not pears,
so wasn't deep enough in his knee-bend
to pass under freely,
his blue mail shirt
like a second sky
swinging up to the branches.

And the pears,
little riddles of women,
gold-green and etch-speckled,
announced themselves
like stealthy percussion,
one fruit plunking
in the mouth of the mailbag
pear Avion.
Warm. Unnoticed.

In the leafy edges of air
the mailman stops,
sidesteps, straightens.

Each pear so unlike
an envelope,
he thinks, as some wait
near his street-worn shoes
and more above him sway.

Yet each arrives
sealed and stored with messages,
one from each seed's letter:
the ripening hope
of trees.

Michael McLane

Sky, Falling

In the darkness, the coyote is easily mistaken for a dog. One forgives the boy for calling him over. In the remote, the boy is easily mistaken for prey calling out its distress. One forgives the coyote's approach. In the midst of the meteor shower all forgive them their battered instincts. They slowly flee for their lives towards one another. The flashbulbs of the world's unraveling record their error. They pass as cars speeding by a crime scene.

Ladies and Gentlemen

there has been an accident. what is there
to say? a man waits on a bridge for a slow
moving train. somewhere in Nevada. it is
broad daylight. he has a firm handshake

and green eyes. some things must be deduced
from a man's resolve. we are all delayed
indefinitely. or is it inevitably? my son used
to make choo choo noises when I'd leave for work.

that is what I told the police. you can see them
out the window to your left. an investigation
into unpaid debts commences. but a man waiting
for a train does not leave a note. he expects to be home soon.

the farms to your right date back to the territorial period.
speaking of which the dining car will close in fifteen minutes.

Settlement

The problem with trees is obscurity. You cannot see your future lumbering through the night towards you until it is already on the roof. So we cut them down and distribute them evenly among us so there can be no blame. And we are many and cold, and the trees are legion. One among us has learned to play music on a saw. Low and trembling.

ARCHIVE

I say blood money when you say collect.
I hand a receipt and a lock tumbles closed.

When *proper burial* is spoken, what is meant
is the etchings roots make as they creep.

This is fine art
this box labeled *correspondence.* All it contains
is private general corporal. Letters.
Address removed. Inscrutable.

I shave my head always over the bathtub
carefully collect my remains. The next day
is the coldest.

Of course, when asked to sharpen a life
we mostly forget to whet it first,
plunge, hope the bones will do the work

Carbon copy.
Provenance.
Certifiable doubt

or small lines that only approach it.
Hold your breath as you run,
then you have the feel.

In one folder, a fingernail. Clipped.
Place it beneath the camera.

Mannequin Wave

The mannequins are waving goodbye, goodbye,
their hands detached from their arms, goodbye.
I've seen better hats in the yard. This hat hardly touches
the ground, fedora, bowler, hat for a shoe man.
The mannequins are waving goodbye. The basil
withers in snow like seaweed or green kale.
The mannequins have someone's hair and mouth.
They are taking the day off with no clothes but a wig
we detect from half a mile and a wink. Here is a wrist
for silver, here a chest for a blouse, goodbye
sawdust heart, goodbye. Our sun is a lesser sun
than the sun for mannequins. Think better,
sweet corruptible, dalliance with the ripening pear.
The mannequin teaches children to wear clothes,
the dress from the "brilliant" designer, the dress
from underwater, empty shells like trumpets,
waves on waves you could never survive
with the skills you were given. Mannequins carry on
without you, like you. When lights go out.
the mannequin stands still amidst the finery,
the jewels the wrist watch, the scarves from Japan.
They are so serene. They know, these mannequins
the lights will go on in the morning. They will be
admired in Kashmir, in their pose that mimics grace
falling through the world. They will last
beyond the temple, beyond the sun they admire.
They hold their hands at the end of their wrists.
The mannequins wave goodbye, and the world
dissolves, sugar and silk sneaking through their brains.

The Dead Go to the Dance Outside of Town

The dead are driving cars. The dead
are sitting in the back seat with jewelry.
The dead are studying optometry, studying
the way to get inside a girl's dress, studying
dancing and moonlight on the river through
Russian olives. The dead are dancing to swing music;

they smell of cologne from Public Drug,
the dead have been drinking though they are
too young to drink, too young to be in love
with the future, though that is all they love.
The dead know the way to Cascade with the lights off,
and the Village Inn. They know what to order
without looking at the menu. The dead have affairs
with the woman in the front seat, though that
is years from now, wives away. What are years,
the dead say. The dead say goodbye to the living,
one of them in the same car with the dead.
The dead stop talking to her, but she keeps
talking to them, telling them the story of their night
but telling no one else, not her children, not her mother
even after she is dead. She tells the dead who lived it,
the dead who are driving away from the dance,
drunk Montana, the highway lit just so far ahead.

Leaving Things

For Sofia

We leave things
        more durable than the body,
ring that tarnishes green
against skin, a pill box
with a blond wing of hair tied with string. Perhaps
there is a license plate, a tie clip, a billfold, a jacket
stored in the closet in plastic so
        moths don't come, don't,
so shaped like him, the suit, shoulders where shoulders
were, invisible heart beneath the lapel. In the hipster's home,
a cocktail glass survives
the bars he drank in,
came to the thrift store amidst football mugs,
anniversary flutes, glass where lips sipped gin.

The things in the lamplight, in the hall, in the light
the sun gives up through windows, sun on the junkyard
where they took the scrap
metal, the fender, hubcaps,
the impact, back wheels, where they took the bills
unpaid the gulls ferried off,

the things, luminous
and unseen. They become
ours if they want to,
things to hold in our hands dissolving around them,
keychain, tiepin, the photo with the kitchen sink,
soon will
        arrive silver drifting silver air,
the letter, cufflinks that fit cuffs of this white shirt,
golden wristwatch losing
minutes every three days,
a gear like a sparrow's tongue with just a breath,
one of his days, lily throat speckled pollen, a voice.

Laura Stott

The Girl With No Hands

stole a silver pear
from his majesty's orchard.
And the gardener saw it, believed
she was an angel.
The way she tilted her head back
and stretched her neck to the sky
to eat. Her hair hung like silk curtains.
And in the moonlight,
how could he not
fall in love with her?
How could he betray this love
and tell this secret
with the time to count each fruit?
Each destined
for their numbering.
It was a story the gardener couldn't
explain, but had to account for.
So, the gardener and the King waited
in hiding for the maiden
and when she appeared, hunger
was in the girl's every step.
They dared not speak,
but watched her, as moths lightly played
around their faces.
Are you of this world?
If I am a dream, then I am a dove.
Be my queen, I will make you hands,
and the gardener wept, and the king
kept what was never his to keep.

The Fall

I ate the apples you've become famous for.
I didn't eat the huckleberries,
I was too late for that.
I did eat the branches, the stems,
the shriveled worms inside them.
If you believe me, I did this.

If you would believe me,
I ate more than the flesh of the apples.
I ate the core,
and the seeds because I am immune.
I ate thorns in the woods,
scraped off their skin with my teeth
and sucked until they grew dull
and swallowed.
Yesterday, I ate the wheat.
If you believe I would,
I picked and ground the wheat myself,
dusted the flour into my green bowl,
baked and ate it for dinner.
I ate the ashes because I cooked them to black
as night,
and then ate the stars.
Except for the poisonous ones,
which I planted,
concealing their bright flesh in yours.

MONSTER

Spider webs by the backdoor funnel into
a black cave, a silk and nocturnal universe
where a fanged creature waits
for the moon's threaded children
—a moth, a mantisfly—
to step gently into the tangle
of reflection.

Mother spider wraps her eight legs lovingly
around all her young and whispers,
this is the earth
you are waiting to be born into—
dream of the wings you'll eat,
and kingdoms between roses.

Amanda Luzzader

Between Places

Jessie knew before I did. "As soon as the door opened," she told me later.

Mom came home early that day. She walked in without seeming to notice us and headed straight for her bedroom. All three of us girls followed, and we watched as she rummaged through a dresser drawer. She unearthed a cigarette—must have squirreled it away when she quit a while back. It quivered between her lips as she lit up. Then she closed her eyes and took a long drag, holding the burn inside for a moment before releasing it in a slow, smoky sigh.

And then I knew, too.

Seven jobs in two years.

The next week I found myself in the backseat of our old Chevy with my older sister Jessie on one side and my younger sister Liza on the other. Our feet competed for space amongst the duffle bags and grocery sacks in which we'd packed all our possessions.

"How long are we going to stay there?" Liza, she was five then, had sunk in her seat until her seatbelt came up to her armpits.

"Not long," Mom answered. "Just while we're in-between places."

"How come you're not staying?" Liza had asked this a half-dozen times, but she kept asking, as if the answer might change.

Mom sighed. "I need some time to figure things out. You guys shouldn't have to deal with my problems."

"Where will you go?" Jessie asked.

"I dunno. Maybe California. Along the coast."

Hours later, as the sun was settled behind the mountains, our car finally hiccupped over the train tracks and we passed into the little town where Grandma and Grandpa lived.

"Can we ride the train to come see you?" I asked.

"I won't be gone that long." Mom glanced back at me through the rearview mirror. "Besides, these tracks aren't used by passenger trains anymore. They're mostly used for freight."

"What's freight?" Liza asked.

"It's like baggage," Jessie said. "Clothes and stuff."

"Could be anything, really," Mom said. "Anything that needs to get somewhere."

Grandma hugged us at the front door. A cough drop clicked against her teeth as she rolled it from cheek to cheek. While Grandpa went outside to get our things, Grandma showed us where we'd be sleeping. Liza was the youngest, so she'd sleep in the room next door to Grandma and Grandpa, in case she got scared. Jessie and I would share the guest room in the basement.

"You'll have to make your own beds," Grandma said. "My hip's too bad to go downstairs anymore."

Jessie and I raced downstairs to inspect our room. Jessie was two years older than me, but she never acted bossy or superior. Before we had reached the bottom step, we were already pretending to be roommates renting our first place. Jessie was only my half sister, but she seemed more than whole to me. I didn't even mind sharing the queen bed with her.

The guest room smelled like an old library stocked with potatoes. A water pipe ran along one of the walls, and when it sang, I'd wrap my hand around it to see if the water was hot or cold. The carpet was pink, and wood paneling lined the walls.

Jessie and I were trying out the bed when Mom appeared in the doorway. She had her purse in one hand and her keys in the other. Jessie and I both sat up.

"This'll be nice." Mom looked around the room as though she'd never seen it before. Then she said, "I'm about to go. Come give me a hug."

Jessie scampered off the bed to embrace her, but I didn't move.

"Aren't you going to hug me goodbye?" she asked with one arm draped over Jessie. There was a hurt in her eyes that guilted me. I crawled off the bed and hugged her tightly at her waist. I kept hugging until she pried me away.

"Tell me when you're coming back," I said.

Mom looked up as she considered the question. "August twentieth," she said. "I'll be back the twentieth."

After she left, I begged Grandma to take the calendar down from the wall. I counted the days. The twentieth was nearly six weeks away.

"I'm going to mark each day until she comes back," I said.

"No, I'm going to," Jessie said.

"What about me?" Liza asked.

Grandma found three different colored pens—red for me, blue for Jessie, and green for Liza—and every morning we'd each cross the day off in our own color.

While we kept careful track of the days, it was harder to track smaller units of time. Grandma and Grandpa didn't use clocks. I never even saw one in the house. Instead, they listened for train whistles. A train told us when it was time for lunch and there was another for dinner. A whistle late in the afternoon told Grandpa when to stop working, and the train that chased the sunlight signaled bedtime. The red-eye came through around 6 a.m., and though I seldom heard it, it woke Grandma and Grandpa each day. We got accustomed to finding them dressed, fed, and waiting for us in the kitchen when we finally rolled out of bed.

One morning, I awoke alone; Jessie was already up. The white curtains over the window glowed with sunlight, and birds whistled outside. Wrapped in the thin quilt, I didn't want to get up. I just stayed there, wondering about Mom. I pictured her at the beach, the wind blowing her wavy hair as she waded into the water. While I daydreamed, my eyes roamed around the room, and suddenly I saw a man's face.

He was in the paneling next to the light switch. The wood grain swirled to perfectly outline a rounded beard and pointy nose. His slight frown and droopy eyes made him look sad. I felt like crying when I saw him. I couldn't help but think he hadn't wanted to be a wall in a dank basement. Of all the things he could be—a throne, a rocking horse, a nativity set—it must have been disappointing to end up as nothing more than a spot on the wall.

At first, I'd have to search for his face, but after a few weeks, I couldn't not see him. I'd squint to change him back to wood, back to grain. But when I'd leave the room, his eyes followed me.

On August thirteenth, I came upstairs to find Jessie helping Grandma fry eggs and toast bread. Grandpa had donned his reading glasses and was perusing the paper while Liza sat in a chair kicking the table. I stood in front of the calendar with my red pen, as I did each morning. Liza's green x's had stopped appearing weeks ago, and Jessie's blue marks stopped shortly after that, making it my job alone to mark the dates leading up to Mom's return. Her phone calls had dwindled from every day to every other day and then down to once a week. But as I crossed off the day, I noticed the date boldly circled in three different colors was only one week away, and my heart fluttered.

I sat in a chair next to Liza and stared out the window at the distant miles of train tracks passing through the fields. I always hoped to see a train while we were waiting for breakfast, but I never did. My grandparents told me that I'd never see one at that time because the trains always stayed on schedule. I wanted them to be wrong. I checked every day, but the tracks were always still and silent—lonely in the interim.

"Do the trains here go to California?" I asked.

"Of course," Grandpa said. "Trains go anywhere there's tracks. These ones connect all the way from Sacramento to Tallahassee. That's clear across the country."

"But they only go on their route," Grandma said. "They can't just go wherever they want, they have to go where they're expected, and I'm not sure that the trains she's seeing go to California."

Grandma set a plate piled with toast on the table, and Liza lifted the corner of the top piece with her pinkie. "Grandma, you burnt the toast."

"Eat up," Grandpa said. "It'll put some hair on your chest."

"I don't want hair on my chest," Liza mumbled.

Grandpa folded his glasses and put them in his shirt pocket. "Do you girls know I brought your Grandma here on the train?"

We did, but we loved to hear him tell the story.

"When was that?" Jessie asked as she pulled up a chair.

"Right after the war. I decided I needed to find a wife. So, I went to the city, found the prettiest gal there, married her, and brought her home. Easy as that."

"I wouldn't have come if I'd known I was coming to this," Grandma said.

Grandpa covered his mouth with his hand, but then whispered loudly, "I wouldn't have brought her if I'd known she'd turn into that."

Grandma hurled a hot pad at Grandpa's head and he laughed.

I tried to picture what Grandma must have looked like when she arrived on the train, back before the wrinkles and extra pounds. The best I could come up with was a life-sized cutout of her black-and-white senior picture that hung in the hall. I imagined Grandpa stepping off the train, and then turning around to help the two-dimensional beauty down the steps and leading her to her new home. In my mind, her picture with its frozen smile, donned an apron and spent the rest of its days farming, washing laundry, cooking and raising six photo paper children. If Grandma had really known what her future held, I wonder if she still would have boarded that train.

"Hey, look! There's Meanie!" Liza jumped from her seat and ran to the window.

None of Grandpa's barn cats were particularly friendly, but Meanie was the white cat from hell. We could sometimes pet the other cats if we got them cornered, but not Meanie. She'd arch her back and puff up so big her tail would look like a raccoon's. Then, she'd bare her teeth while hissing and spitting. If we still didn't leave, she'd fold her ears back and a scream would escape her open mouth, as if our mere presence was exorcising some demon within.

"Her kittens should be getting big enough that she'll bring 'em down soon," Grandpa said.

When the time came for Meanie to have her kittens, she'd climbed up to the rafters of Grandpa's barn—too high for us to see her babies.

"Why'd she have them up there anyway?" Liza asked.

"Probably to keep them away from you." Grandpa laughed.

"She'll either bring them down soon or they'll fall and break their necks," Grandma said.

Grandma's comment had us girls going to the barn every day looking for raining kittens so we could rescue them. Sometimes we heard mewing, and we'd stretch our hands above our heads hoping to catch them. Grandpa would walk by and say, "Just promise me you won't handle them too much. They'll get soft and won't make good mousers if you touch them too much."

The week passed with no sight of kittens, but by then we had other things to think about. On August twentieth, we girls unrolled several feet of butcher paper in the driveway. Jessie brought out her portable radio and while the Beach Boys sang, "I wish they all could be California girls," we decorated the banner for Mom.

I wanted it to say, *Welcome Home Mom!* but Jessie said we needed to write Welcome Back since this wasn't really our home. We settled on *Welcome Mom! We missed you!* but we ran out of room for the longer phrase and had to write the "you" in small print vertically at the end of the sign. Using crayons and markers we added hearts, stars, and rainbows to the banner. The texture of the cement pressed through the paper where we drew, and Liza ripped a small hole on the left side, but it still looked pretty good. When we were done, Grandpa got out his ladder and hung the banner outside above the front window.

"She'll be able to see it from a mile away." He smiled.

We girls went inside and stood at the window, watching for our car to bring Mom back to us.

"A watched pot never boils," Grandma said, and she ushered us outside to play. As I ducked out the back door, I caught her looking out the window herself, staring down the road.

A little while later, Grandpa asked me to go grocery shopping with him.

"What should we get to eat to celebrate your Mom coming back," he asked as he pushed the cart past the milk aisle.

I almost said sausage dogs, 'cause they're my favorite, but then I thought about Mom and decided to get her favorites instead. We bought ribs, corn on the cob, potatoes, and a nice, big watermelon.

Long after the evening train's whistle sounded, we girls sat on the couch with our pajamas on and our teeth brushed. Grandma sat in her rocking chair holding her old rotary phone on her lap as the chirps of crickets floated through an open window.

"I guess we oughta get you girls to bed," Grandpa said.

Liza's eyes were already drooping and she didn't seem to be aware of anything. Jessie and I looked to Grandma as Grandpa carried Liza to her bed.

"Well, who knows when she'll get here," Grandma said. "Just get to bed, and we can all have breakfast together in the morning."

We went downstairs and lay in our bed. I tried to stay awake in the darkness, ears straining to hear the car's motor or the front door open, but despite my resistance, I fell asleep.

Jessie and I woke up at about the same time. We looked at each other, and then flew upstairs, but when we got there, we only saw Grandma and Grandpa.

"She isn't here," Grandma said. The wrinkles on her face looked deeper. She wrung a tissue in her hands. "I just hope she's held up somewhere and hasn't gotten in some accident."

It rained that day in big swollen drops. The water dripped off the roof and emptied from the rain spout like a faucet. Jessie, Liza, and I stood in Grandma's living room in front of the window, watching the rain and checking the road. The raindrops made the marker run on our banner. The colors swirled and dripped off the sign like colored tears.

Grandma stepped behind us and gazed over our heads and out the window. She walked away silently, and then suddenly appeared outside the window in the rain, without her jacket. She lifted her kitchen broom with both arms and swatted at the banner as her underarms shook. The paper ripped, part of it wrapping around the broom. She lowered her arms, and the entire banner fell to the ground. She looked up at the window—we made eye contact for a just a moment—and then she turned and walked back toward the garage.

All three of us ran to meet her at the door. When she swung it open and saw us, she stepped back in surprise. The rain had drenched her clothing; I could see her bra through her plaid shirt. She stepped past us, still holding the broom.

"We'll make a new one tomorrow," she said.

Grandma and Grandpa spent a lot of time on the phone. I kept marking the calendar. I couldn't shake the feeling that if one of us didn't cross off the days, Mom would never come back.

A few days after the rainstorm, we were playing UNO downstairs. I came up to get some graham crackers for a snack and overheard Grandma speaking sharply on the telephone.

"—School will be starting soon. You can't be like this when you have children. They need to have some stability—"

I ran back down the stairs, jumping over the last three steps.

"Grandma's talking to Mom!"

I turned and raced back up the stairs with my sisters at my heels. We rushed to where Grandma was pacing with the receiver. She'd walk about five steps before the cord reached its limit, and then she'd turn and walk the opposite way. Grandma didn't even seem to notice we were there until she nearly collided with Liza.

"Call me tomorrow, and we'll figure it out. Your girls want to talk to you."

Grandma handed the receiver to Liza. "Hi, Mommy," she said cheerfully. Without giving our mother a chance to respond, Liza started telling her about the kittens in the barn.

"Where has she been?" I asked Grandma while Liza talked. I'd had a nightmare that Mom had driven our old Chevy off a cliff and into the Pacific Ocean.

Grandma shook her head slightly. "She's just been busy, that's all. Nothing to worry about."

Liza didn't stay on the phone long; Jessie took her turn next. After they talked for a while, Jessie handed the phone to me before heading back to the kitchen.

"Hello?"

"Hi, Sweetie! How are you doing?"

I wrapped the phone cord around my pinkie. "Fine."

"I knew you'd have so much fun there. But I miss you so much; I can't wait to see you girls again."

"When are you coming back?"

"Oh shoot, Honey! I can't really talk anymore. I'll call back tomorrow. Love you! Bye!"

The phone clicked before I even got to say good-bye. I stared at the receiver a moment, and when I looked up, I saw Grandma watching me. She took the handset from me and placed it back on the cradle.

"She sure seemed to miss you." Grandma smiled, but her eyes didn't wrinkle the way they normally did. "It'll only be a couple more days now."

When the train whistle blew for supper that evening, we sat down to a meal of ribs, corn on the cob, mashed potatoes, and watermelon for dessert.

After dinner, I went to my room to put on my shoes so I could check the barn again for kittens. But just as I was leaving, the wood grain man caught my eye. Though I heard nothing, I sensed him calling me. Jessie walked in and caught me staring at him.

"What are you doing?"

"Who's that crazy artist that cut off his own ear?"

"Van Gogh?"

"Yeah. This mark looks like his face."

She moved beside me, both of us facing the wall.

"I don't see anything."

I pointed. "It's right here. See, his face is turned like this." I mimicked his pose, and even lowered my eyebrows and exaggerated a frown. "You don't see it?"

Jessie shook her head and walked out of the room.

The grain man was emboldened now, nearly coming out of the wall.

I found a pencil and I traced the lines, pressing so hard that lead dust sprinkled to the floor. I moved over and over the wood grain, bringing to life his eyes, his mouth, his nose, and especially his one ear.

When I finished, you couldn't even tell I'd traced it. It looked like something an adult had drawn. Like a Van Gogh. I stepped back admiring him; he wasn't just a part of the wall anymore. Now he was somebody.

Next to the face, I signed my name in big capital letters, knowing Jessie couldn't miss him now. I went outside to get her, and found her next door in front of Grandpa's barn. I forgot the drawing when I saw two kittens cradled close to her chest.

"You caught 'em?"

The kittens struggled in Jessie's arms; she could barely contain them.

"Here," she said, "Take one."

"Hi there little kitty. What's your name?" I cupped my hands under the kitten's soft creamy fur, holding him close to my stomach. The kitten purred and rubbed his head against my hand as I pet him. Even though he had the same coloring and similar markings, it was hard to believe something so precious had come from an animal so vile as old Meanie. I wondered if Meanie had once been like the kitten, and if the kitten was destined to be like Meanie.

I remembered what Grandpa had said about not handling the kittens too much or they wouldn't be good mousers. Meanie was a great mouser. I quickly stroked the kitten's fur and rubbed my cheek against his side.

"I don't care if you are a lousy mouser," I told him as I carried him to the house.

On the bed in our room, I dangled my hair in front of the kitten and laughed as he swatted at it.

Liza heard me and ran in. "A kitten!" She gasped and jumped on the bed. "I want to play with it."

I scooped him up. "You can play with it when I'm done," I said.

She watched as I caressed the kitten's head.

"Can I have a turn now?"

"Not yet."

I nuzzled his nose, rubbed under his chin.

"You're not supposed to have pets in the house," she said.

"Shut up, Liza."

"When do I get to have a turn?"

I rubbed the cat's ears. Twirled its tail around my finger. Liza sighed and stamped out of the room.

But almost as soon as she left, the kitten began mewing. It became unruly, slipping through my arms, rolling out of my hands.

"There, there, kitty. She's gone now. Don't worry. I'll take care of you."

The mewing continued.

The kitten escaped my grasp, jumping to the bed where it assumed a very strange pose.

Uh-oh.

I smelled it before I saw it.

"On the bedspread?" My grandmother with her arthritic hip loomed at the doorway, a scowl deepening her wrinkles. Liza stood at her side. "Get that cat out of here before I wring its little neck."

She turned to leave the room, and as she did, she saw it. My masterpiece. My Van Gogh. From behind her, I watched her fingers curl into fists. She pounded the wall three times. "Dammit, dammit, dammit."

She whipped back. "You're ruining my house. You're ruining everything! You're just like your mother!"

I picked up the kitten, ducked past Grandma, and ran up the stairs two at a time. Grandma was your standard-issue, cookie-baking, choir-singing, white-haired grandma. I didn't know she could swear. Her words reverberated in my mind.

In the backyard, the swinging gate's old hinges squeaked as I stepped into Grandpa's farmland. The kitten freed itself from my arms as I reached the barn, but I kept walking.

My bare feet curled around hardened lumps of soil. Strings from my cut-off shorts tickled my knees.

The sun, lingering near the horizon, beckoned with yellow light that seemed somehow truer than that of noonday. The sun kissed the world with Midas lips. It converted my brown hair into shiny threads of Rumpelstiltskin gold, and warmed my pale skin.

I walked farther than I'd gone before. Too far to hear shouts to come home, and still I walked. I walked until I reached the end of Grandpa's farm, marked by a crooked fence of sticks and barbed wire.

Beyond the fence, within a stone's throw, I saw pebbles leading to creosote-stained wooden ties and rusting railroad tracks. My eyes followed the line for miles, all the way to the center of town where a familiar, mustard-and-maroon Union Pacific engine stood parked with its line of freight.

Its whistle bellowed as the train lumbered down the tracks.

A calling came from within me.

Race the train.

My heart thumped inside my chest. I turned parallel to the tracks, waiting to start. The whistles sounded again. The ground vibrated. The tracks clanged.

The train sped past, its thunder blowing through me. And then I ran—arms pumping, legs galloping. I watched the train with side-eyes, my hair a spiraling smoke trail behind me. The air tried to force me back, but I pushed through, and when the train dropped behind my view I knew it was chasing me. I was the conductor of my own train then, unbound by the limits of tracks. I could go anywhere, see anything, and I ran, smiling, ahead of the train.

But then my feet slowed, and my arms dropped to my side. A fence squared off Grandpa's property, stopping me. There was no stopping the train. It barreled onward, snaking around turns and climbing up hills, charging ahead to the places it was meant to go, stopping only where it was expected to be. It left me behind in the dust and smoke, somewhere between places.

Natalie Taylor

Miscarriage

My daughter orders air
plants from Belize, Honduras, Peru.
They pile outside in crisp
brown boxes until she slices
tape and lifts them in her palm
to inspect. Smaller than her thumb.
Ounces, if that. They don't need soil.

Their spines, curled like octopus tentacles,
reach and stay as if movement
dictated form.
The base more bulb than root.

She builds a shelf from a kit.
Hammers tiny brass nails into pre-
cut rectangles. Tries glue.
Abandons the project.
Leaves the hammer, glue, instructions
next to the stereo
speakers and subwoofers someone gave
her for when she moves out.

Lines the plants up on the coffee table.
Carries them to the greenhouse.
Instagrams them.
Carries them to the bathtub
where they float
until we have to shower.

In between Japanese anime and Skyrim
battles, Googles *tillandsia*. Buys a special
watering can with a plastic orange
hand pump and adjustable
nozzle that delivers precisely the right spray.

Installs them in two sets of wire baskets.
Hangs them on the front porch.
Worries about sunburn.

Adjusts location for optimal
indirect sunlight.

One day she shows me a blossom
like a red flare. It's a pup.
She explains the mother
plant will stand guard until
it is ready to hold its own. But

I am only half listening. I am
thinking of the baby she lost.
How she said she didn't know
what to do with the clotted
tissue undulating like a dim
anemone in the toilet.

Do I try to hold it?
A red pup rooted to air.

IF YOU DON'T COUNT

My cat, 22 and senile,
wakes me up every
morning by doing laps.
Jumps over my head
like a small panther stealing dreams,
crop dusting me with farts
reeking of leaking bile,
lands with a *humpf*.
Jumps off one side of the bed,
humpfs, prowls around the
foot of the bed until one of her
remaining claws snags on the carpet.
Frees herself, heaves up. She
weighs ounces, how can she
be so loud?
Over my head. 4:30.

The house is her litter box.
Gray feces squish between my toes
when I walk in the dark.

If you don't count
vomit and the tumor,
hard as a lime between
her breasts, she shows no
age. Glossy black fur,
eyes yellow as a reason.

She still surprises me:
wrecked bones, shattered moth wings,
squirrel's tail.
I tried to kill her.

One morning, waking to rotten
stench of that tumor,
shit in the bathtub,
I put her in my car,
drove to the dog park,
carried her to the tunnel,
under a grove of weed trees,
and threw her into the
heart of the shadows.

I went home to rest.
It rained then. Of course.
And the first real cold of fall.
So I took a can of food and sat under the
Cottonwoods, watching a pierced kid in black
leather throw Frisbees for her retriever.
When it missed, the dingy
fangs clicked into place.

The next night,
I put salmon in gravy
right next to the first can
dried now, and untouched
on the side of the cement,
called her name into the
black tunnel.

The third night I brought
Bumble Bee solid white albacore.
Recited: Kids,
I'm really, really sorry,
I know how much you loved her...

It was after midnight before
I heard her trilling
from across the other side
of the street like some dark diva
that had just landed from a quick
trip to Thailand and couldn't
wait to tell me about the appalling
sleeping conditions.
Hungry, but otherwise completely
intact. If anything, more alive.

Anne Shifrer

White Robin

we could only see her tail,
a few white feathers poking out
from the nest, like a champagne flute,
ethereal—not the sturdy gray
of your standard bird

chance we spotted her
chance she was white
and yet her little furnace
worked—to keep her there,
steady, with humans so near

it's hard to imagine birds
mating, much less this pretty ghost
of one elected from the lawn-hopping
worm-eaters, nature's chosen

white flower, white spider, white moth—
Frost saw them, the miniature evils
of design—but something must be
right somewhere, permitting
such waywardness, white robin,

blue eggs

Dippers

They post themselves on rocks in the river
then bop up and down like mechanical toys
made to charm children.

No one knows why they do it.
Maybe they dip to triangulate
positions of prey—that place
in the water that pauses a little
with an insect's whirring around
both with and against the flow,
an ampersand in the river's onwardness.

They stand as if glued to the rock
until suddenly they're off
so fast, an unseeable moment,
when they shoot out

and into the water, using their wings
as flippers or fins to finagle
their way downriver, snagging a bug
on the way in a beakful of water.

They're gone. And we realize the roar
of the river, the almost haunted space
of where the dipper once was.

Then we see them downstream
on another rock, hunching their bebop
shoulders and peering into the fluent and chill
convolutions of their river world
while we upstream feel the emptiness,
the lightness, the leaven of wonder.

Ben Gunsberg

RHAPSODY FOR A TRAPPED AMERICAN GOLDFINCH

How long must I watch him strobe
the ceiling of my garage
like the wild eye of a child's flashlight?

Shouldn't he be flitting an Aspen grove
or throwing his lemon-bright stitchery
against a white stucco church?

Can't he see the clouds and hear the trills,
sense the junipers shoulder up
to dusk, bees sizzling round the porch?

And doesn't he have a song for dusk,
spreading overhead like a slate terrace,
smudging out the day's raggy shadows?

Is he waiting for the sun to belly under
so he can fine-tune
a preamble to the knuckling rain?

Surely the moon will call him out
once the sky darkens and stretches
its gloom-rich resin.

Then again, he may seek
more than relief from heat,
something splendid and articulate,

like an albatross tilting toward Alaska,
lulling the wind with Emersonian
lectures on the life long-lifted.

Or has he entered my garage to remind me
that among these practical American tools
a restless animal forever circulates?

Is he a symbol I can look through
like a lens, or a metaphor for desire,
or some other swooping abstraction,

swooping inside a tight two-car garage,
where my mind tethers to the tight
two-car circumference of his flight?

As long as we're attached, shouldn't we float
like breeze-bounced spores
or find a fence to jackknife?

We might drizzle down the Delaware,
unreel our wooings by that water,
beside those throaty steel mills.

An old owl splashes his pinions there
and claims the whole country
once sparkled like Jerusalem,

every leaf tremble, every bus and beggar,
every millstoned thought of a new world
once hot as an oil drum campfire.

Are you the pilgrim I would be,
searching for seeds, breadcrumbs, dew drops,
if not for this sensible garage?

Fleeting shadow on the cinderblock wall
who twines my vision with a strangled
frenzy of wings, go now. Take me with you.

Machine Overheard Teaching Boy to Read

What is in the mitten   click on
the question mark   that's right
a question mark shows what is in the mitten
click on the skunk
down by the words   the mitten
rewritten   go on   practice reading
this page   click on the rewind button
repeat   what is in the mitten
great   now you can play it back
click on *what*   this is not the word
what   click on *what*   that's right
click on *in*   click on *in*

click on correct   click on *mitten*
this is what sentences should look like
click here   this is not the word mouse
a mouse is in the mitten
which of these words goes in this
blank   that's right   a mouse is
in the mitten   the sentence should
say a mouse is in the mitten   correct
a porcupine is in the mitten   that's right
a porcupine is in the mitten
you got it   a porcupine
is in the mitten   that's right
the sentence should say
what is in the mitten   the sentence should
say   click here   the sentence should
say   click on the pencil when you are finished
correct   you made a great story.

Kase Johnstun

The Push

On my mom's bookshelf sits a dark yellow picture. She stands with frizzy hair, brown shirt, and green bell-bottoms behind an old Formica kitchen bar. In front of the bar, my cousins and I sit on stools. We are children – we range from ages three to twelve. Jake and Judd fight over one stool while Kelly leans forward with his tongue sticking out. Mikelle sits daintily on a stool of her own while Tara holds a tiny three-year-old me on her lap; my OshKosh B'gosh overalls stand out red and bright against the faded yellow hue of the 30-year-old photo. We smile. We sit at my grandma's house just down the road from our own in the valley beneath the looming mountains of Northern Utah – her house, the thick family adhesive. The faded picture reveals a sibling-like relationship among cousins, one held together for decades by my mom and her sisters.

Wimp, wuss, chicken – these three words boiled my blood. And my sibling-like cousins and especially my brother liked to use them a lot when they referred to the youngest boy of the group – me. There were no niceties put on between us, and on the living room couch, a week before our family's week-long trip to Lava Hot Springs, Idaho, I had guts, enough guts to agree to jump off the first tower at the Lava Hot Springs pool. And I told them so.

Between 10 and 30 people, spread out in age between four and 45, would make the short trek every summer to the tiny town at the base of the towering Rockies. The whole crew shared a one-bedroom apartment – adults got the beds and the kids got the floor, the tub, or the grass outside the condo. My mom and aunts spiked our Sprites to ensure a nice evening.

Lava didn't only take us away from the monotony of summer but gave our parents the week-long retreat they needed. It took them away from their offices, their waitress gigs, their cranes. In the days before internet and cell phones, they couldn't bring their work with them like we do now. When they departed the work site or office, they left it behind. They couldn't burden their kids with business calls during dinner or text messages before bed or email checks in the morning before the day could begin. When we got our parents away from work, we got all of them, and they got all of us.

The last 20 miles of State Road 30 that leads to the village winds through tall canyons and along the Salmon River. The miles went so slowly. Jake and I huddled between my parents who sat in the bucket seats of an old, full-sized brown Bronco. In those days seat belts laws and parents were more relaxed. My eyes scanned the valley between peaks to see the towers pop up on the horizon. With no three-story building in the town, the tower served as the focus of the Lava Hot Springs skyline.

"Five dollars to whoever spots the tower first," Dad would shout out when we got within a few miles. Five dollars at the pool might as well been a million.

The amount of soda, candy bars, or video games five dollars bought in the early eighties rocked, but you had to spot the tower to get it.

Jake and I stared at the shifting horizon. We watched for that concrete tower, which Jake always spotted it first, a fact that pisses me off to this day, more than two decades later.

My cousins and I woke way too early for a facility that opened at 10 am. We paraded around all corners of the condo only wearing swimsuits and holding the four dollars for entrance, wadded up in one hand and a towel in the other. Kelly jumped right off the balcony to get out first and the rest of us took the boring stairs after our moms snagged our trunks and yanked us down off the edge of the ledge.

Year after year, our parents couldn't hold us back from running across the stretch of open grass at 9:30 a.m., just to arrive at the entrance one minute later. So we sat and waited in line for 29 minutes for the attendants to open the gates and let us into the locker room doors. We ignored the tiny sign that told us to shower off before entering the water; Doctor Brown from *Back to the Future* said, "Marty, where we're going, we don't need roads," and we said, "where we were going, we don't need showers."

My confidence from the week before did not follow me to the pool, but Jake's grasp on the elastic of my shorts did.

We started to climb the ladder straight up; it seemed to me to be up, up, up, and more up. After a few rungs, I looked down, and saw with great relief that no kids climbed behind me. The option to back out existed. With Jake above me, I stepped down a rung. But a giant teenager stepped onto the ladder below me. I was stuck.

Jake stood on the first tower and looked down at the gap between us. I followed him to his summer briar patch, a place where he and my older male cousins flourished for one week every year. I turned toward the long, rectangular, and Astroturf-covered slab that hung over the pool. My body stood paralyzed until the teenager behind me moved me closer to the edge. He no doubt headed to the third platform that stood 33-feet above the water, a place of unimaginable fear.

My feet felt the cold, wet concrete beneath them. Eight or nine kids stood in line to jump. Another boy stood in fear. He shivered with his arms crossed in front of him. His older sister stood behind him. She put her hand on his shivering back and said something like "it will be okay" or that "I was scared my first time too." He turned his face up to her and smiled, his body moved with confidence, and when the lifeguard signaled a one with his finger, the boy jumped instantly. Proof of his existence after his jump was nonexistent.

"Come on, wimp," Jake said. He looked back at his skinny little brother who had more visible bone than muscle on his body and whose ribs stuck out like speed bumps for trickling sweat. He stared at my eyes and in them he saw my fear. His arm flung itself around me, and when I expected to hear that it would be okay and that he was scared his first time too, he shoved me in front of him and said, "You're not backing out of this, wimp." Without my mom and dad's threats, he would have tossed me with pacifier still in mouth.

My cousin Judd stepped behind me in line. Bastard. More pressure. I had to jump now. Had to. Jake knew me, knew my fears, but now I had to jump to be cool.

"Everyone's watching," Judd said. He pointed off the tower toward the entire Cordova clan.

At the top of the tower, fifteen feet in the air and getting ready to jump, I gripped the guard rail on the left hand side of the deck. My oldest cousin, Kelly, flipped in the air toward the pool. Our corner contingent sprawled out on the green lawn that wrapped itself around the pool. Our picnic baskets and towels sat right at the deep end.

I imagined how my mom would feel if her son's last moment came because of his older brother's taunts – the last look on his face smeared with fear. In photos taken in Hawaii a couple years earlier, I lay on a boogie board crying, staying out of the shark-infested waters while my mom, dad, and brother took photos beneath the water with their thumbs up and their snorkel gear fully submerged.

Every couple minutes the lifeguard made it through the rotation of jumpers. And every couple minutes Jake and I slowly shifted toward the front of the line. My family lost interest – the older girls returned to sun bathing, the younger kids returned to the kiddy pool, and mothers and aunts returned to their books. My turn to jump came.

The moment Jake's body flew off the 15-foot high tower, the moment his feet left the green Astroturf, the moment his toes no longer touched the Olympic diving tower, I knew I shouldn't have pushed him. He fell toward the water – hard. It's a simple law: little brothers do not push bigger, stronger brothers off high towers. A second earlier, the lifeguard's index finger went up. I panicked. My hands grabbed Jake's shoulders and swung him around until he flew off the platform. His eyes looked back at me in mid-air before he dropped. He tried to dive in but didn't have enough time and could only turn slightly sideways before he splatted on the surface of the water. He frog swam to the edge. His hair split at the part with each push. Then he surfaced like a pissed-off submarine of revenge. His eyes found mine the moment his soaked hair crested the blue, and they followed me until he cleared the edge of the pool where he disappeared from sight. He had begun to climb the stairs, he had brought his friend vengeance, and it would only be moments before he killed his little brother. In a second's time, he would weave through the line of kids waiting behind me. He wouldn't care what the lifeguard said and wouldn't care if he got kicked out of the pool. He would find me on the ledge and obsessive prodding would be replaced by brute force.

At the top of the ladder, Jake's head popped up. His nose, his chin, his shoulders, his elbows, and, eventually, his little-brother-pushing hands came into view.

The lifeguard raised his single index finger and yelled up to me to go ahead. Their system seemed so simple. It kept kids from smacking each other mid-air or landing on each other's heads in the pool, and it worked the majority of the time.

The system was fantastic and flawless when thoughts of death did not thicken the air.

Jake's body approached, and as he shoved the first little boy out of his way and his hand landed firmly on the second little boy to clear a path, I did what I had tried to avoid for the last 20 minutes. I walked toward the edge of the tower and then walked off. To everyone watching, including my mom who decided to look up at that exact moment, they saw a tiny E.T. like figure walk off the edge of the platform, turn in mid-air and while dropping, grab the edge. Two tooth-pick arms held on while tiny chicken legs flailed with the breeze. The lifeguard yelled. People gasped. With no lifeguard law, kids flew off the platforms. Flailing bodies almost hit me on their way down.

I held on as tightly as I could. My eight-year-old fingers grasped as much of the platform as they could until a couple of feet stepped right next to my fingers – one hand let go and then the other. I spun downward toward the concrete edge of the pool then swam to the top of the water, where the lifeguard pulled me out by my arms. Both he and my mother began to yell, but the adrenaline dulled their voices.

"If you would have hit your head during my watch, I would have been fired!" the lifeguard said.

"Okay, sorry."

"Sorry is not enough. Head straight to the condo!" my mom yelled. Then she pointed across the lawn toward our balcony and pushed my back in that direction. "One hour, mister."

"One hour?" I whined. An hour at the condo at Lava Hot Springs seemed like for-ev-er, to steal a line from *The Sandlot*. My cousins ran around, jumped, jumped off, waded, slid, bounced, dove, and ate under the sun and mountain tops. The clock's big and small hand slowly circumnavigated the tiny circle. It was unbearable. So I jumped on the bed in my parents' room, and the smell of the polyester, cotton-blend blankets calmed me.

The clock made its final tick of the hour. I threw my towel back over my shoulders, sprinted down the concrete stairs, ran as fast as I could across the grass along the fence, flashed my wrist badge, ran along the poolside, climbed the tower stairs, stepped onto the green carpet at the end of the platform, waited for the lifeguard's finger, and jumped as high and as far as I could into the deepest part of the pool, whizzing with joy in the air and splashing down hard and fast.

I didn't know as I lay there on the bed and waited for the time to go by that that week at Lava would be one of the last times we would all caravan up to the middle of Idaho together, one of the last times we searched for towers, ate pizza and ice cream after full days in the sun, rested quietly on the lawn, looked up at the stars, and played kick the can until being told to shut up by a crusty old lady who hated my family and all the kids.

Since then there have been four exes, a couple of psychotic boyfriends, DUIs, jail time, stabbings, abundant alcoholism, and lost jobs. Since then there have been 12 beautiful children brought into the clan and so many baseball games, days at the lake, barbecues, first days of kindergarten, and even graduations and marriages. Since then and even more so after my grandmother's death and then my grandfather's, we dispersed. Since those last few summers in Lava, in the most common manner, our lives opened to the fates of adulthood, the grasps of soured relationships, the slugs of pain – the global shards of fragility that are flung when the glass door of innocence breaks.

Twenty years later, I stood at the edge of a balcony again and looked out at all my family watching. They sat and stared at me. They stared to see if I could go through with it. They had all gotten married long before.

Jake stood behind me. With a tiny flask of whiskey and asked, "Need some of this?"

"I think I would throw it up," I said.

Sometime after my brother's best-man speech and before the traditional rolling on the river to CCR's "Proud Mary," my mom snagged the six of us and led us to the stairs outside the reception hall. She held up the old, yellow, and now-torn photo taken years ago and touched each of our shoulders to gently nudge us into position. We sat in the same order as we did 30 years ago, each faking protest but then settling in to smile at the camera. Our photographer took the photo quickly. He knew the bar was open and beckoned and that we all needed to rejoin the party. We dispersed from the stairs back to our separate tables. When I got the photo a couple months later, the creases had found their way around our mouths and foreheads and the yellow peered out from the corners of our eyes.

Carrie Cannon Scheidel

Nobody Likes the Elderly

for Ma and Pa

The air will get close and heavy in the house
And we will learn that you cannot be trusted
To switch off the burner under the teapot, or even to stick around.
You will realize you have the wrong limbs, wrong faces
And that some of your parts will come off or out,
Which you will ask us to retrieve for you from containers.

The old fevered battle of love-making is reduced
to a low-grade bicker.

Her jaw will thicken like his;
His thighs will soften like hers.
The chlorophyll of manners will drain into the ground,
Revealing that the yellow of annoyance, the orange of disgust,
And the red of rage were always there.
Then we will place our hands on the clammy backs of your necks:
You will recognize that you no longer belong here.

Scoliosis

Had God been at all square with us, the quadrants of her back
would divide as logically as the Four Corners. And had her spine followed
the easy cartography of the desert,
she would have walked that line all the way from Dinosaur, Colorado
to Rodeo, New Mexico. However, in this land, where smallpox blankets were
gifts
and innocents were shackled to fields,
Her backbone cut into her like the writhing Rio Grande. So to save her, to
standardize her,
men weld heavy rebar to the bone. A brutal blessing.
Or this new hardware is railroad track: a means to a bright, modern era,
the low Western sun stinging her eyes.

THE STARVING

started with the tiny silver key, which went down like a Necco wafer.
Her papers were now safe from Mother.

A few months later, she worked an entire spool of thread down her esophagus.
It was a blue that had been discontinued.

The bar of soap she bit off in chunks. The bitterness was awful,
It reminded her of penance.

The hairbrush tickled her throat so much it hurt, and tasted of the lubricant
Mother used
In her old Singer.

She chewed the red chair Father made for her childhood,
A relief once it was out of sight.

The old Schwinn took just one day. It took three days to rub the last black chain
mark
Off her chin.

Surprising how easy it was to get the old Monson building into her gut
     It left dust on her tongue and staples in her teeth.

It was even easier to swallow the vast sky. She could breathe a little
With it swelling in her.

After consuming the dogs and trees and people, she sank her teeth into her own
arm
     And kept starving--

OCTOPUS'S GARDEN, IN THE SHADE

My Sweet, I will suck each millionth mouth, grit my teeth
    as your eight dreaded arms tangle me
    in love. You taste every touch.
My Alien, your head holds three hearts, which twitch in triplets for me—
    your head, too, has its wheel-within-a-wheel, revolving with
    the image of a glass bottle in the swell, which you let go simply to catch
again.
My Love, you are infinity on its side, a whirling dervish of scythes, a figure on
the ice
My Mushroom, blue and boneless, I am breathless.

Chadd VanZanten

Just Wait for the Answer

This girl is so quiet. You may have misjudged just how quiet she really is. There are things you know about her, things you don't. She listens to classical music, can ride a horse. Ambivalent about seafood. Trivia, mostly. There is one thing you know for sure, that she's quiet, but there's nothing you can do about that now. Your time is up.

She puts on her coat and together you go out into the night and the rain in the parking lot.

"Tonight was great," you tell her.

The girl nods and grins. That's all she does.

The asphalt shines in the darkness like a great spill of ink. You walk her to the car and open the door and she gets in. Rush around to the other side and you get in.

Streetlamps glimmer wet and bleary through the windows. For a few seconds you don't look over. She's there in the passenger seat and you figure maybe she'll say something if you can keep yourself from looking over.

But she doesn't, and so you do, and when your eyes meet, she turns away. There is no more than eight inches separating the two of you, no sound but the rain. It makes a noise like radio static.

You start up the car, but it doesn't seem to fill up the quiet, so you begin to talk at her, and you keep talking for a while.

"Sure got cold in a hurry. It was gorgeous this afternoon."

She peers up through the window at the wet black sky as if to confirm this.

"My stupid car," you continue, "it fogs up so bad. I'm sorry." You wipe the windshield with your palm, then switch on the defroster. "I have to run the defrost and the AC together when it's like this."

"Mm."

"Yeah, the evaporator fins in the AC unit condense the moisture out of the air, like a dehumidifier. It's a trick I learned. See, it's already starting to work. There's really not much difference between a dehumidifier and an air condition-er."

You're not entirely sure if that's true.

She laughs. You know of no sound you would rather listen to. Hearing it makes you laugh. Then you both sit quietly again in the watery light as the defroster breathes a rough and continuous sigh.

The car idles. A raindrop creeps down from the top edge of the windshield, joining with nearby droplets until it becomes a rivulet that courses down and out of sight like a tear. This girl has said nothing and is apparently content to keep doing so. You gnaw at the inside of your cheek to stop yourself from lecturing further on the physics of automobile climate control.

Maybe a laugh or a glance from this girl holds more meaning than that of another. You recalibrate. Because there's something you plan to say to her. Something heavy.

You love the girl.

She probably knows, but it's time you said it to her. You rehearsed it earlier so that it will come out right. It didn't go very well. It felt dishonest to manufacture a moment between two people, to force it into the open that way. But you wanted it to happen right, and so you practiced, and now you're gauging the mood. And you want to know how she'll answer, so you're trying to find the right place to begin, like a pilot reading the wind and searching for somewhere to land. You scan the landscape. The landscape of her.

"You know, I was surprised," you tell her. "I never thought you'd be into a stupid movie like that one."

She shifts in her seat. Or maybe that was a shrug or some cryptic utterance of body language that you failed to catch.

"It was fun," she admits. She looks at you.

"Right, it wasn't too bad. The movie, I mean. It was okay."

"Yeah. It really was."

"So," you breathe. "Tomorrow."

She only nods. But when you look at her she doesn't turn away. You turn in your seat to face her, turn off the car and defroster, and remove your hat.

You speak her name. Then you tell her, "I love you. I do. And I've been wanting to say it."

Then you nod. Once. As if to punctuate it. As if to let her know that you're through speaking for the time being. Or maybe forever—at this point it's hard to say. Because it didn't come out exactly the way you rehearsed. There was something you wanted to say beforehand, to transition into it. There was a cadence to it. But the moment has been created and it begins to unfold around you. And it unfolds around the girl. She played a role in it, is still playing a role. And so you discover that any such moment must be forced into existence, or else it couldn't exist at all. Like a line of words in a love letter, or a parting embrace—they are intentional acts to be held between two people, even if only for a short time.

The girl puts her face in her hand and cries. She cries because she leaves tomorrow. In the morning, she'll be gone and you will likely never be together again. You haven't decided what this means or what can be done about it. So, you take her in your arms and hold her, and you keep holding her for a while. She squeezes you hard, buries her face in your shirt. You breathe in the smell of her and pull her softness against you.

Through her sobs she whispers your name and you feel it on your neck.

If you lose her, it will be months before you appreciate the cost of it, and the pain will last much longer. Some of it will never go away. But there is one more thing you learn in the dim light of that inky parking lot: love is a girl sobbing on your neck, and the price of love is loneliness.

When the girl settles back into the passenger seat, your shoulder is damp. She sniffs, wipes her face with her fingertips, and says nothing. All is quiet but for the rain. It streaks the windows. Your cheeks grow hot and you watch the girl for signs.

She sits still, arms folded across her middle. Her back is straight, head tilted forward. On her face an expression that is neither smile nor frown. You cannot see her eyes beneath her long eyelashes. If there is any signal in her stillness, you lack the ability to infer it.

Then she looks up. Her arms unfold and her hands come to rest in her lap, one soft petal cradled in the other. Her gaze meets yours and her lips part. She draws a breath, and if you thought what you had to say was heavy, just you wait for the answer.

Marianne Hales Harding

CONFESSION

I have sent many a man to hell over the years

More when I had a size zero body
a suede miniskirt
coordinating leather boots with stiletto heels

but even now,
with a pair of Spanx and a foundation of slimming black,
I can inspire an impure thought or two

As a child I deduced that I was responsible
for my own thoughts and actions
because blaming my brother
never got me off the hook

But I learned better when I grew into womanhood's superhuman powers:

Without lifting a finger
I can sully a man's thoughts
Without breaking a sweat
I can turn a pious man into a covenant breaker
Without a single utterance
       I can stir a man to action
All the catalyst he needs is my presence
He isn't in a position to refuse me

Oh, he tries.

But his fate is as sealed as
a drunk girl's at a frat house
He's about as safe
as a prostitute who changes her mind
It's no wonder he's as skittish
as a 13 year old girl sharing a bed with her mother's boyfriend

He must feel so
       violated
He must wish he had
       control over his own body

How angry he must be, waiting for me to
        take responsibility for my actions
and
        stop making him the bad guy
We all know who's at fault here.

On the Condition of Being Dead

When I am whittled down to 20 letters and 16 numbers
on a modest stone that still costs
more than ought to be spent
because in their grief
they couldn't resist the tiny etching
that hinted at my artistic flare,
stop by on occasion
and leave an inside joke
in the overgrown grass
to catch the eye of those who wander by
and make them wonder
what happened in the years
that passed between the two dates.
Maybe leave a verse or two
(if you are feeling financially reckless, carve it in stone).
Make it the sort of poem that expands
in the mind like a child's bath toy
so I can spring up, full sized, for a few squishy moments before
drying out and returning to 20 letters and 16 numbers
in a silent sea of dry-eyed stone.

Dianne Hardy

LOT

He left her there, a pillar of salt
To the mountains he did flee
With two virgin daughters scrambling behind
As God said it should be.

T'was a cave in the hills they did find
A place where they could stay
Lot left the girls to tidy up
While he went out to pray.

"Poor Daddy," said one girl to the other
"This really is quite a plight,
Our mother's a statue of salt back there
With whom can Dad spend the night?"

"I think it's my call to do the Lord's work
It's my right, I'm older than you.
When he drinks this wine he'll lie with me
You can have him when I get through."

An orgy raged on the mountain that night
Each gal played her part to the letter.
In drunken splendor Lot climaxed it all
"Wife, you get better and better."

Then the Lord looked down and said to Lot
"Look, these daughters you've defiled,
You're righteous and you're clever too
Through each will come a child.

This story is one not told in church
In the Bible you'll need to look,
Revelation, scripture, from the pen of God,
It's the world's first dirty book.

Susan (Nyikos) Pesti-Strobel

DRESSED TO KILL IN SMALL TOWN, UTAH

Salute to Kim Addonizio

I'm putting on that little black dress.
        Walk down Main Street every hairline wrinkle
                showing in my cleavage endless like time.
That little dress   sleeveless   backless
        tight like armor. Oh, how the ruffles flirt
             and veil my weathered knees! And yes
every strand of hair shaved to a stump
        a showstopper for sure   just look at
             the green wave from north to south
no one   no crossing   can stop me. Blank greeting cards
        sigh and wave from the Hallmark shop window   the ones
             never sent to me and I don't care.

By the sports goods store prime bicycles
        sparkle in a chorus line   front wheels turn
             to follow my little black march and I'll keep
walking even if
        this is my last stretch
             under stealthy looks shot
from idle eyes hooded in family vans
        eyes my spike heels might just gouge out
             eyes starved for steamy sidewalk dreams
modest shorts aching
        to drop behind the butcher shop
             where I order tongue and tenderloin.
And how that blue-eyed butcher longs to wrap me
        in crackling sheets of paper
             hairs standing to attention on his beefy forearm.

I might just die and be buried in this little black dress.

And the band will play on
        and we will all paddle to this other world
             across a sizzling Styx of haute coffee. Black. No cream. No suga'.

IN BED WITH BILLY COLLINS

For a week now each night he takes off
another piece of clothing – I know
he does that from time to time –
peels off a frayed sweater, unbuttons
all seven four-holed shiny white buttons
of a gossamer oxford shirt, though maybe

the top three were already left undone
to cleave a clever view of a mussed
garden of sweaty chest hair.

Then dimming corduroy pants slip
down into a breathless accordion to halo
vales and peaks of ankles so fragile
that my hands yearn to cup
them like a child's frosty face
after a lost snowball fight.

You will want to know
that all this time he is standing
there next to me—I in my bed—looking
a little puzzled as if he has forgotten
my name and many others
possibly worth forgetting.

One look stops
my yearning hand from touching
him or his now puddling clothes
and he trots off to take
a bath in a claw-footed bathtub
while I turn the page.

Then he puts on a robe, his skin
still steamy and fragrant underneath,
maybe lavender or magnolia,
his cheeks open like pages,
calls me *you* as we sit
opposite at an orphan kitchen table downing
hot leafy tea on Sunday morning
before this something between us ignites
the F pages of his shelved encyclopedia.

He writes my name
into a faux-paradelle, nothing
personal, it seems, and at least
he does not remember me as a hippo
though he could have, and he could,
any minute now, unfasten
that threadbare bathrobe and maybe one of us will,
right after *picnic! lightning!* loose that first
"Oh, My God!"

Later, I wrote in a notebook
it was like riding a 1941 Nash
Ambassador, but that's all I can tell.

RAISING HIM/BEST ADVICE

If he is hungry he will eat
If he is tired he will sleep
If your milk dries up drink this tea
            three times a day
If he has fever   make a poultice
                        bathe him in cooling water
                        make him drink this
If he coughs all night rub mustard
                        lard
                        lemon
                  on his scarred chest
If he cries never ever pick him up
If he falls into a coma sing to him
If he recovers from surgery
                  behind schedule
never ever stay with him 24/7

If he learns
            to walk three days before
            his second birthday
            will a girlfriend care?

Raise him as if nothing's wrong with him.

If in PE that kid kicks him in the forehead
which swells up like a beehive
never ever sue the school

If he can't keep up
with his brothers
      in math, English, science
just push him harder
Do not hold him back a year
Do not hurt his father's ego

If he doesn't learn to drive
    by twenty-six
    but moves back in with you
If he growls no can do, no can do
If he quits job after job after job
If he cuts, cuts, cuts, 1" apart
If he skips therapy

You'll know what to do.

Daniel Nyikos

Potato Soup

I set up my computer and webcam in the kitchen
so I can ask my mother's and aunt's advice
as I cook soup for the first time alone.
My mother is in Utah. My aunt is in Hungary.
I show the onions to my mother with the webcam.
"Cut them smaller," she advises.
"You only need a taste."
I chop potatoes as the onions fry in my pan.
When I say I have no paprika to add to the broth,
they argue whether it can be called potato soup.
My mother says it will be white potato soup,
my aunt says potato soup must be red.
When I add sliced peppers, I ask many times
if I should put the water in now,
but they both say to wait until I add the potatoes.
I add Polish sausage because I can't find Hungarian,
and I cook it so long the potatoes fall apart.
"You've made stew," my mother says
when I hold up the whole pot to the camera.
They laugh and say I must get married soon.
I turn off the computer and eat alone.

Felicia Rose

THE MOSAIC

The café evoked a certain ideal. Tucked into a narrow cobblestone street, it abutted a tiny bread bakery on the one side and an even smaller shoe repair shop on the other. Inside, dim light emitted from Moroccan fixtures. A stained glass transom above the door opened at an angle allowing into the café a hint of air, if not of light. Mahogany church pews lined the two side walls and several mosaic-tiled tables stood along them. Wire-backed chairs completed the seating. A Strauss opera was playing from a small radio above the espresso maker. It was a Sunday afternoon and so the performance was being recorded live.

Larissa hung her raincoat over her arm and sidled into a narrow seat on one of the pews. She removed a small, hard-covered journal from her handbag, noting as she did, the faint dirt stains beneath her nails. That morning in the hotel room she'd scrubbed them, but to no avail. I wonder if I give myself away, she wrote. No matter, I suppose. Though for memory's sake, I'd like to pass. She described the woman sitting to her left, mid-fifties, like her, fit, well-dressed in a tailored skirt suit and sweater, her chin-length hair stylishly cut. Her fingernails looked clean. She was reading Barthes, and appeared engaged.

So, too, did the pale-skinned youngster with dark black hair, long on the one side, short on the other, who was reading Proust. Larissa glanced at the youngster, at the exposed silver pipes along the walls and at the painting of a pastoral scene involving mountains and streams. How, Larissa wondered, did all of those elements, disparate though they were, accord? Yet, accord, they did. She lifted her espresso, imbibed its aroma, sipped it, and then returned the demitasse to its saucer. In this micro-world of the café, all of the elements fit together as in the opera that was playing: the dim lighting, the demitasse cups hanging on narrow iron racks above the barista, the casual way in which the two black-clad waiters brought customers their drinks, and then returned to the Sunday Times crossword puzzle they were doing.

An apparent ease permeated the place, the way in which the barista, the waiters and the customers alike seemed to belong to the same world, to know their roles. Larissa imagined their lives branching seamlessly from beyond the café: the woman beside her discussing Barthes with her students, the youngster with the asymmetrical hair reading until the wee hours in a tiny bare-floored room, the two hipsters with their tight black jeans, wool caps and stylishly tattered scarves repairing to a design studio with the blueprints they had sketched.

The clothes they were wearing now would carry them into the university, the studio, the opera or back to the café. Each of their lives seemed to form a unified whole. And though each had a different function from the other, all, like the instruments and voices in the opera, united to harmonious effect. One would no sooner add Bongo drums to a Strauss composition than a goatherd, replete with straw and stench, to the café.

That the hipsters had ink on their hands contributed to the ease with which they fit in. It suggested what? That they belonged to the urban art world. Dressed as they were, they might even work as baristas or waiters to support themselves as artists. Not so the woman to Larissa's left, though she might have in earlier years. She, no doubt, spent time at dinner parties and bookstores and Parisian cafes.

Larissa considered her own attire: a dark wool skirt which skimmed the top of her knees, and black suede boots which skimmed the bottom; a burgundy wool sweater, hip length, fitted; a scarf. Just the day before, the scarf had lain in a bin at a thrift shop, itself, like the café, small, darkly-colored, dimly lit. Strewn atop a pile of other wearable items, the scarf drew her attention. Its vintage burgundy and hunter green floral hinted at an earlier life draped across a woman who might frequent operas or cafes. Larissa had bought it along with the sweater, skirt and boots and the narrow leather handbag she held in her lap. Dressed thus, she felt harmony with her surroundings, and even, for the moment, with her sense of self as urbane, a reader of Barthes and The New York Times, a patron of opera as she had been the previous night.

And yet, a nagging feeling ensued that she was part of a stage set, that someone had dressed her thus to play a role, that, let's say, of a Bohemian intellectual or, if one assumed her clothes to be new instead of used, a well-to-do middle aged woman who could do as she pleased and so chose on this Sunday afternoon to dress up and come to this Italian café where she could write in her journal and listen to German opera and delight in the pleasure of bitter espresso.

All of which heightened her sense, not merely of playing a role, but of being an imposter. For truth be told, nowadays, she wore mostly coveralls and thermals. Her work demanded it. It demanded, too, that she begin her chores before dawn, which she did seven mornings a week, but not before brewing a strong cup of what her neighbors referred to as cowboy coffee.

The barista came around the counter to sit with the waiters. His long white apron reminded Larissa of her college days some thirty years earlier working as a short-order cook. She liked the physicality of the work, deep-frying the julienned potatoes, flipping burgers on the grill. But each shift had left her smelling of grease, which only with difficulty could she remove from her body and not at all from her clothes. Her roommate, a French major, shelved books in the library, and got Larissa a job doing the same. Larissa enjoyed wearing neatly-pressed skirts instead of oily jeans, pulling her hair back in a bun instead of tucking it under a white paper cap. Yet, she chafed against the drudgery of having to apply her thoughts to reading the call numbers on the books, and then finding their appropriate places on the shelves. At least in the cafeteria, her mind could wander, unencumbered by the necessity of focusing on tedious tasks.

Later, as a copy editor, interesting reading material sometimes came her way. But often, tedium prevailed, and she found herself dreaming of doing physical labor out of doors instead of mental labor in a windowless office. Sometimes, she'd find herself gazing at the watercolor of a barn in snow she'd hung above her desk. Reveries of tapping maple trees or tending livestock occupied her thoughts. Gradually, her style changed. First, she gave up heels. Then she replaced the suits with sweaters and jeans. Finally, one day, to the raised eyebrows of her colleagues and boss, she wore coveralls to work. Her sartorial transformation complete, she created a life to match it.

At the age of fifty-two, after thirty-one years of editing copy, she submitted her resignation. "You're demoting yourself," her boss said. "And for what? To become a shepherd and carry a staff." Larissa refrained from saying it was not a shepherd she was planning to become, nor did she admit she'd rather carry a staff than continue to be part of one. Instead, she nodded. And then, with every cent she'd saved during those years, she bought a ranch and seventeen goats.

Not once did she regret her decision. Seldom had she even thought of her old life, except with a sense of gratitude for having left it. At first, she'd considered editing copy from home, but then she learned to make cheese, which she sold to neighbors, and eventually to a food cooperative in the city. She'd come to the city now at the invitation of that cooperative, where, the next day, she'd speak about her goats and her farm. She'd demonstrate how to make goat cheese. She'd wear flannel-lined jeans, thermals, an apron. She'd look like the farmer she was.

Outside, the sun was setting. The waiters lit candles. A middle-aged black man wearing a beret sat where the hipsters had been, took out a copy of Nietzsche, and read. I wonder if he'll be wearing the same hat tomorrow, she wrote in her journal. The candle on her table flickered, then held steady, illuminating the table's mosaic. The apparent randomness of the overlay intrigued her: green, brown and gray-blue tiles, some triangular, others curved, still others a combination of both. One purple tile, mostly triangular, but with a curved hypotenuse, lay along the edge. The pieces didn't exactly match, but somehow they fit. Thus it is with the soul. Larissa thought fondly of milking her goats, making the cheese. Then she ordered another espresso, wrapped the scarf around her shoulders and took out a book.

Nancy Takacs

The Worrier

freesia

What does it look like?

Mango and apple
in tiger skin,
a lily tongue.

What does it say?

"In a warm field
shadowed by Monarchs
I glowed with rain.

I could be perfect now,
flicker the way
with my cardinal wings."

Why a cardinal?

A cardinal once lit
on the clothesline
as my mother and I
argued, scattering
donuts to the birds.

We kept looking
into the pines
for those bright wings
to stop us.

What did you hear?

We listened to its what cheer?
and what we thought
was—love you I love you.

What is the freesia's question?

A ripe grape
with many seeds.

What is the answer?

My right hand,
freckled and willing.

What have you learned?

To be curious,
silent. I want to open.
I want to be red
but hidden.

When I lick a petal
I lighten my tongue
with sugar and crumbs.

What have you learned?

I could be perfect
now.

LEAVING FOR TWO WEEKS

—for Jan

You unlock the cinnamon ferns, chickadees,
unlock the gold centers and quiet moth wings,
unlock the wish of entire, unlock skim and hum.

The sky a quilt-wheel, yesterday a mirror of hemlock.
You want the day of peacock chants,
a whip-poor-will that used to call from our elderberry.

You have that farmhouse aura inside skyscraper.
You were right about Perfect. But then
the edges have aroused denim.

I've filled up on strawberry and chive,
the crush of hull and stem almost unnerving.

I have your yellow flannel still in my back seat.
When I get back, you'll wear it on a porch
where they let you smoke.

Vanilla and lavender tapioca some night,
mock meat balls in rum.

You know how to rest the stems of asters,
you know when to bring
the blue hydrangeas in.

John Kippen

TAROT

think of something you want to know
pierce the unknown with a query
ease your anxious mind with tarot

will I end up with so and so
settle down and have a baby
think of something you want to know

how long will I be stuck in Reno
should I join the nunnery
ease your anxious mind with tarot

would I enjoy living in Ontario
can I trade my sister for a pony
think of something you want to know

should I buy a Honda or a Volvo
what might be the outcome of surgery
ease your anxious mind with tarot

will I ever look good in a speedo
should I join the military
think of something you want to know
ease your anxious mind with tarot

OUIJA DREAM

the board glows green
planchette drifts

words bent by turns
emerge, blue polyester

white frizzy curls
and a red shirt

she asks about my mom and my cousin
tells me about a shell she found in Peru

ribbon fish dangle from her lamp
casting shadows on a tabloid

Migraine

snagged by an
    unseen assailant

black tendrils through hair

he hides

desperate, I ingest
                      an eraser

pink square
in search
  of smoke

the result:
dirty pilings   and

a smudge

Philip Parisi

Garlic

Yesterday I ripped you from the ground,
tied you up and hung you
in the garage to dry.
This morning when I opened the door,
you bowled me over with your thick accent,
mugged me with your little pungent knuckles.
You screamed your protest
in the only language you know
right to the root.

Your feisty small fry riot
made me chuckle the way we laugh at tiny guard dogs.
But you must be tamed.
I put you in a box and shut the lid,
put you in the garden shed and locked the door,
left you in solitary confinement to calm down.

In time you will learn to reserve your powers,
redirect your energies for another season—
in my stew.
But, I know that in the end,
at a delicate moment
when my guard is down
your ghost will have the last laugh,
your revenge
lingering on my breath.

Bucket List

I'd like to visit all the fruit stands
on Fruit Way gorge on the visual abundance
of purple eggplants, sweet peppers, squash, and the cucumbers,
mix with the people scurrying eagerly about,
feel up the peaches.

I'd like to crawl through the Utah's slot canyons,
bungie jump off the Temple Towers,
hang glide over Manhattan,

eat untainted fish,
drink guiltless wine,
and paint the wide open spaces with the pigment
of eternity.

Run myself to exhaustion
in all the marathons to promote healthy breasts.
Help a victim of a suicide bombing.
Rescue the buckled-up children from the van

of a mad mother who drives into the ocean
at Daytona Beach.

Spend a cozy night alone
with Pussy Riot
in a Russian jail cell
thumbing our noses at dictators.

Raise up for a moment the
women bent over in the fertile valleys
picking my recommended daily servings
and say thank you.
Meet a child prodigy and converse
about what universe he came from.
Slap a child molester in the face.

Join the Muslim women protesting
in the streets of Cairo,
lift their veils and kiss them
on the cheek with a hug.
And if my bucket overfloweth,
I'll give it a swift kick into next lifetime.

Charles Waugh

The Folly of Crows

Spotting a shred of reflected light on the ground below, the crow descends. His discovery is better than he first imagined: not just a shred but a dense crumpled ball of aluminum foil, slugs of chicken grease escaping the tiny crevices, the careless remainder of some recent picnic feast. Grasping it tightly, he leaps away, his flight cloaked by the bickering of passing grackles.

His mate has some luck as well, though not quite as good. A shiny, but useless gum wrapper atop an open garbage bin brings her attention to a square of foil, red in splotches from tomato paste. Alone in the dirty alleyway, she examines it on the spot, removing bits of sauce. Satisfied, she too grasps her prize tightly, returning home, anonymous.

All afternoon, they scour the city, collecting each find at their treetop lair, where they smooth and sort the piles by size. When night falls they have all the foil they need, and in the secretive dark, they pinch and mold the scraps into place.

At the morning sun's first glimmer, life sparks within the firebird and a blaze bursts forth from every glinting feather. Rising into the wind, it flaps its brilliant wings, scattering drops of molten light, blinding the crows. Undaunted, they imagine every offspring fulfills its destiny with an instinctual sense of self, an intuited understanding of its parents' hopes and dreams. In subdued whispers, they reassure one another that junior can do little else but seize his imperative, ascend the firmament, and with fiery blasts purify the world before plunging, extinguished, into the sea.

But the firebird, spiraling gracefully skyward on a thermal of compassion, simply calls to his parents below—Haw! Haw! Haw! —and soars.

Tim Keller

The Gift

Mom usually begins her Christmas shopping in June, but this year she announced she would no longer buy presents for all the children, grandchildren, and great grandchildren. Instead, she would take down Dad's life story and use the installments as gifts for the family.

Secretly, I and everyone in the family considered this something of a holiday foul, but the folks are long retired now and as the family has grown, the time and expense of shopping for everyone has gotten prohibitive. So, we all smiled and nodded politely.

Only I suspected the truth—that Mom would nag Dad until he finally deigned to speak. She would then write his every utterance in longhand until her arthritic fingers could take no more, and leave the resulting hieroglyphs for me to decipher.

When she brought me the notebook to transcribe, it was all I could do not to groan. Except for a list of titles ("My First Horse," "My Trip to the Dentist," "The Old Yellow School House"), the pad was empty. I realized that, in addition to my own holiday and writing responsibilities, I could now look forward to— this.

Mom must have read the frustration in my expression because the next words out or her mouth were: "Your father is a great man."

It's a familiar refrain. What's more, it's true. Stalwart and glacially calm, his moral compass reliable as true north, Dad's an exemplar of his generation, but though I love him dearly, we've rarely seen eye to eye.

Dad was born a middle-aged conservative who took his seat on the high council the moment he left the womb. I, on the other hand, am impulsive and ruled by passion. We get along all right around other people, but alone, we're sort of like two old Tom cats circling in an alley.

"I know," I assured her. "It's just, do you want to write it down for me?" I asked hopefully. "Then, I could, you know, edit it. That way, it would sound like Dad was doing the telling."

"No," said Mom, "I want you to give it some style. You know, write it like one of your books or something."

Wonderful, I thought, pulling out my laptop. *The gift that keeps on taking.*

"Yeah," Dad said with an amused snort. "Style me up."

"Dear," said Mom in that special tone of hers, the one that says *proceed at your own peril*. "Dear, I know you think this is silly, but it will save us over two thousand dollars in gifts this year alone. So, you can take this seriously or you can break out the checkbook and start writing."

I started up the laptop, sat on the sofa facing Dad's chair, and waited smiling. Mom had us trapped and we knew it. Dad grunted a begrudging affirmative, cleared his throat and began to speak.

* * *

I grew up during the Great Depression and my family was large, even by the standard of the day. Then again, people didn't worry about things like that back then. Yes, more kids meant more mouths to feed, but they also meant more help around the farm. Families took care of each other in those days, you see.

With four older brothers and four older sisters, I was the baby of the family. Which meant that Mother and my sisters spoiled me rotten, while the older boys had to do the heavy farm work. The only bad part was that everything I owned used to belong to someone else! I got two new pairs of pants a year—a church pair on Christmas and Levis for school on my birthday. Everything else was a hand-me-down, including my horse.

Buttons became mine by default. She was too old to carry anyone else in the family, but I was only six years old at the time. I couldn't lift the saddle to put on her, nor could I reach her head to bridle her, but to the family's amazement, I could call and over to the fence she'd come. I would give her some oats, climb the fence, slip onto her back, and off we'd go.

This went on until my mother saw. That's when Papa, (at Mama's insistence,) taught me how to wrap a rope around Buttons' head and neck. Just like that, I was the only boy in all of Mink Creek with his very own horse. She would take me over Devils Hill to Grandma Christensen's for a cookie, or over Jensen Hill to the hot springs with my buddies.

We were just little kids but folks didn't worry like they do today, and our parents all knew—old Buttons looked out for us. Like the time my friend Arlen told us they had baby geese at their place and we should all come see. His daddy told him to stay away from them, but they were only geese. So, we rode Buttons over to his place and slid off her to see the geese.

"They can already swim," he told me.

Of course I didn't believe him. Surely they were too young.

"They can," he insisted. "Help me chase 'em to the creek and I'll prove it."

So, we rounded 'em up and were headin' em to the creek when the mother geese turned and came at us. Their necks were craned forward, wings outstretched, and they honked so loud it hurt our ears. The lead one flew up, grabbed my nose and beat me with its wings. I started screaming. I thought they were going to kill us.

Old Buttons came charging to the rescue. Her first pass sent geese and feathers everywhere. She stood between them and us and reared up, beating the air with her hooves. It was an awesome sight for us little kids.

The geese beat a hasty retreat and they were the last geese I ever bothered. Word got around that Buttons had saved us and we were famous.

She was as faithful a companion as a boy ever had, but as I grew up, her coat grew spotty and she developed a deep bow in her back. As a pure-bred quarter horse, she'd once been the fastest in the territory. Now she could barely lope. Buttons was still a great friend, but she just wasn't fancy to a bunch of eleven-year-olds no longer afraid of geese, (not much, anyway).

So, Buttons and I went from famous to infamous, though anyone who said as much could (and often did,) end up with a black eye, and much as I loved her, even I had to admit she was an old nag. I begged my father for another horse, a real horse, maybe even a thoroughbred. But it was the Depression. We had work horses and Buttons. My brothers had to ride the Clydesdales, Dad reminded me. He said I should be grateful and I knew he was right. If I wanted a horse of my own, I would have to think of a way to get it myself.

I wracked my brain trying to figure that one out. I was heartsick. I had five dollars saved up, but I wanted a horse like the one I saw at the county fair that summer. The old Johnson ranch got foreclosed on that year. A California dude bought it at auction and started trucking in livestock. The first time any of us ran into him was at the county fair, where he showed up with King, the most magnificent horse I'd ever laid eyes on. Horses like that went for hundreds of dollars or more, even in those days.

King was an enormous white stallion, both good natured and fast! He passed all the locals like they were standing still. What with my appreciation for fine horse flesh, seeing that animal made it all the worse. There was no way I could afford even a regular horse, much less a magnificent steed like him. I was already doing all the work I could fit into a day, doing chores and hauling hay at home, then doing odd jobs for the neighbors.

I worked and prayed, prayed and worked and, as always happens when you do your part, inspiration came.

That night at dinner, I asked Papa, "If I can find a way to get my own horse, can I keep him?"

My brothers all laughed at me and I turned red, but I was determined to have my answer.

"Sounds fair to me," he said, as Mama hushed my brothers up.

I set to work the very next day.

The Anderson family owned a big dairy back then and, in fact, their land bordered the old Johnson ranch. This was before milking machines, and the cows had to be milked twice a day. No one wanted to work at the dairy. It was hot and dirty work, especially in the summer. So, when I asked Mr. Anderson if he needed any help, he hired me on the spot, leaving only Mama to convince. She seemed to sense the urgency of my need and, to my great surprise, even let me out of church for the whole summer.

It was hard work, all right. Every day I rode Buttons over to Anderson's before first light and led her up the hill to the pasture.

It wasn't too bad in the morning. The cows would be waiting patiently by the barn door, and the family of cats we'd give the occasional squirt, lined the wall. We'd run the cows in, two at a time, milk 'em, dump the bucket in to the milk cans, run 'em out and do two more. I'd go back up between milkings to get Buttons, ride home exhausted, do my chores there, and then ride back up.

The afternoon milking was a different story. We had to fight the cows, the heat, and the flies. Even the cats'd be gone. The hotter the day the thicker the flies, and when the cows couldn't swish them off fast enough with their tails, they'd head for the creek and run through the brush to get 'em off. Then Buttons and I'd have to ride down there and drive 'em back.

Come Friday, I'd get paid five whole dollars for the week. I was too tired to ever spend it and it wasn't the money I was after, anyhow.

Fall rolled around and back to school and church I went. Every morning I rushed through my chores so I could sneak Buttons some extra oats, apples, and carrots from Mama's kitchen.

By Thanksgiving old Buttons had a certain glow about her. By Christmas she was downright fat, and my brothers Paul and Ronald, the businessmen of the family, were suspicious. One day they stood by the pasture fence, arguing about whether Buttons could be pregnant, vying for the colt just in case she was.

"She's my horse" I reminded them.

"I'm older," Ronald told me. "You can have my Clydesdale."

"Hell, that horse ain't pregnant," Paul opined. "She's just fat."

"Thing's ready for the glue factory if she ain't," Ronald said.

That made my blood boil. My plan, all my hard work—I could feel it all slipping away. Much to my shame, my eyes started to water.

"It's my horse and my colt!" I declared.

"What you gonna do, baby boy? Cry?" Ronald asked, and shoved me away.

We were taught to love each other, and we really did, but ashamed as I am to admit it, at that moment I hated him.

"She's mine!" I screamed, jumping on his back.

Ronald was seventeen and real strong, but I wrapped my legs around him, sank my teeth into his neck and held on for dear life.

He shook and bellered until Papa came and pried me off.

Ronald jumped up and looked to come after me, but a single, particularly expressive snort from Buttons bought me a head start. I ran screaming into the house and hid in my room. Mad and embarrassed, Ronald gave chase, but Mama met him at the door while my eldest sister Velma followed me to my room.

I broke down and told her the story; how I'd rode Buttons over to the Anderson's in the mornings, and pastured her right next to the old Johnson place. Once there, I simply unhooked the fence wires to let Buttons in with King.

The look on Velma's face made me suddenly very nervous.

"What?" I asked. I'd grown up on stories about how they shot horse thieves on sight. "She had to eat too, didn't she? It wasn't stealing, exactly. I mean, King was the one who took care of business, after all."

Velma laughed, and I knew I'd be okay.

"Before long, Buttons had a boyfriend," I told Velma. "And when she started kicking at King a few weeks later, I knew the deed was done."

Velma called Mama, and I'd just got through relating the story to her when Papa, Paul, and a bloodied-up Ronald came in.

"Why did you bite your brother?" Papa growled.

"Adam Archibald Keller!"

My mother rarely called my father by name, and in all my life I'd never heard her use all three; it certainly got his attention.

"That horse is his and that colt is his! You gave him your word, and that's one promise I aim to make sure you keep!"

Not to be outdone, my father shouted, "Has this whole danged family gone nuts? Good hell, woman, that thing's 'bout as pregnant as I am."

You could hardly blame him. It's not every day you see a twenty-five-year-old mare on a farm full of geldings catch pregnant. Talk about Immaculate Conception.

"Then you'd better stock up on saltines and hot towels," Mama said, "because Leness has a story to tell you."

By the time I was done, order was restored and everyone was in good spirits. Everyone but Ronald, anyhow, and even he settled down, eventually.

Papa made me go see Mr. Johnson, who'd stayed on the land as the ranch foreman. I admitted what I'd done and had to work for him every day of Christmas vacation, but I didn't mind.

On a blustery April afternoon, Buttons gave birth to the most beautiful little filly I've seen before or since. Very light palomino with a star on her head and four stocking feet. Between me, Buttons, and my sisters, no horse was ever loved more. The girls called her Kate, but being a boy, I named her Skyrocket.

Buttons died peacefully a couple of years later and Papa died of cancer a year after that. The sale of Skyrocket's foals helped us keep the family farm. Years later I said a tearful goodbye to Skyrocket as we sold her to pay for my mission to Georgia. Mama never told anyone, but she put what she didn't use in savings bonds and when I got back from Korea, she cashed them out to help with my first house.

* * *

I typed furiously, trying desperately to capture the moment, when I realized the room had gone quiet. Only the whir of the fan on my laptop and the ticking of the clock could be heard. I looked up to find Dad staring off into space, his eyes moist.

"Wait, Skyrocket?" I asked. "You called Queenie Skyrocket, and Kate before her."

"Every horse since Buttons," he said. Then he picked up the newspaper and I could tell we were done.

I gazed at him like a stranger. There sat my father, an old and honorable man, to be sure, but for the first time, I also saw a twelve-year-old boy, sneaking his ancient mare through a fence.

Isaac Timm

Sunday Morning

North side of Kings Canyon,
Route 50, a semi-truck burns
like a paper lantern,
aluminum sides flaking
into the sky, leaving behind
the trailer's red bones.

Half-a-mile away
in the radiant heat of ground zero
four of us stand solemn. I look up
at my grandfather, his face rapt
like a man catching the glimpse
of a burlesque dancer's thigh
under a gas light.

Next to my dad stands the truck driver
knotting a corduroy hat
in his hands, mumbling, chatting,
"Oh, God. Oh, sweet Jesus. Oh, God
Oh, sweet Jesus…"

We watch black smoke make early night,
painting the sun red
like Revelations.

Icarus 1981

Seventeen years
his father's pride.

Oh, God
how the girls

would sigh.
As he moved

driven like
Alexander.

Boy not made
for this dusty

dead end, where
nothing flies

but his black
and gold

Trans-Am.

400 cubic inches,
factory prime.

Divine Firebird
pulls easily,

its chariot
past 85.

Smile on
his face.

Hand on his
thigh.

But the desert
tells the truth

well before
it tells a lie.

One blink
turns gravel

into sky.

Oh, God
The sun is

too high.
They say

it rolled four
times

before it came
to rest

his body
thrown

broken on
the earth.

They push
his car

into a pit
for it

had cost his
life.

As far as
I know

It lays there
still,

body rusting
next to

fire.

Dead Camaros

I know a yard
where dead Camaros lie,
saw them crawl in like sick dinosaurs,
gurgling and panting, their mouths
pried open, hands run down their flanks,
sad shakes of the head as blood
drained into pans.

There is no funeral just
summer looting, rims and carburetors,
feet and tongues,

but they are still red, lurking
among the calla lilies and high
prairie grass, longing
to attack the road.

THE YOUTH OF JULY

Girl of fifteen hangs out
the window, slender arm
waving like a moth
at a friend passing or past.
Her escort a phantom young
man from the nose down, eyes
lost to the glare.

The street flows with the
youth of July, some to
eddy into parking lots, pieces
of green yard, spread on
blankets, piled on tailgates.
Laughter, like bells over bass
caught in small moments between
the passing of cars, a cavalcade
of tanned elbows and flashing
faces under a halo of bangs.
Pretty smiling girls to be lost
then discovered. Passing
and turning, crossing in and out
of lanes.

Sex rumbles in the heart like
an engine, a slow present
backbeat happening below sheltering
cottonwoods, under lap throws,
flush young faces, fumbling
hands, groping as if ecstasy
can be lost, to flow endlessly
to the east out of town, with
honking traffic and now headlights.

Evening casts itself out. Beer
cans come out of hiding. From
under daddy's gun rack, from

behind mama's quilt, down
on the floor board. And they drink
until midnight, until dispersed
by unseen hands. Replaced by
empty street, a single slow
squad car, neon that winks
"closed." But somewhere is
a rumble under the street lamps,
the promise of another Friday night.

Charles Potts

Sport Utility Poem

We're in trouble.
Car trouble.

America had a love affair with the automobile
And got knocked up.

Now these little metal bastards are everywhere.

Jerry VanIeperen

Unsought Baptisms and a Broken Coffee Pot

Will they remove me
from the state
if I suggest
gay marriages for the dead?

To offset the ethereal
pluckings from patches
of bright daffodils. An estuary
for a sun in the irrational world.

And night begins slowly
to resemble separate
beings in the reflections
of cracked glass.

Somewhere after death
and the pillow I fall on
my dad lost his cane.
I'm hopeful but uncertain
how to approach the grave.

It's ok to piss outside
when the toilet
is two floors up. It's late.

I don't want anybody
to be upset with me,
coffee pots are affordable.

Think of a rational, functional place
then watch it be wrecked
by unseen interference,
a sunstorm heard across the radio.

The Happy Parade

will be televised nationwide
through generous donations

of corporations and foundations,
with blimps and drones and there's
juggling clowns and dancing bears,
everyone marching, blowing kisses.

It's a celebration.

Then who will clean
all the horse shit and ticker tape
when the storms of confetti end?

Every route ends but the band
freestyles through the graveyard.
We remember the dead, somewhere
have written down all they said,
sometimes we don't even resent them,
let their pallbearers rip cotton candy
away from the grasps of kids.

It's the happy parade
but conscience, or ghosts,
rattle chains in street rhythms
with faces absent, heads down
tattered in cloaks and hoods;
we salute the flags
of a fleet too long at sea.

Somewhere in Nebraska

My body is full
of indulgence. Weak sins,
last night's alcohol
swallowed in this fragile,
twig world.

Langan says there's a carport,
it's got to come down.

The owner is bed struck,
bound in a Yankees jersey,
Gehrig across the back,
impossible to see.

His name is Dan.
A big fucker too, Langan says,
looked like Magnum PI.

We arrive. I can only look
at the sheets so white over Dan.
Who washes, how often
how long?

On the gravel and tar roof
above the cars
even the bugs spin
in unnatural motions.
Last night torments,
a pyramid stuck forever
in sunny weather.

A snake slithers
out of the grass near the house,
Nebraska will not be still,
a harvest of brittle crop. The snake
gains its bearings
I lose mine.

When the carport is broken
I study under my fingernails,
thinking of the origins of cement,
staying in place.

From the passenger seat
I try to drive the conversation
to love or basketball.

I watch Nebraska
beyond Langan
out the driver's window,
I've never been here before.

Langan says
write a poem,
make it your obituary.

Brock Dethier

Across the Grid

They find you easily in Smalltown Utah,
streets radiating in a grid from Center and Main--
First East, First South, First West, First North.
A guy who knew how to handle a mortar
could land a shell on 538 W. 200 N.
without ever visiting the neighborhood.
They know just from your address
who your neighbors are,
your ward and stake,
whose primary your kids should attend.
Handmade signs on your route to work
announce Enrichment,
who's holding the neighborhood no-potluck.
The bus driver, the rural route carrier, the sheriff
know you because they don't see your car on Sunday.

The only diagonal, Boulevard,
hugs the rim of the ancient gravel bench
deposited before Brigham Young's boys
laid down their grid.
People who live below
worry about mudslides,
cars rolling down the bank.
I take it every day,
veering off on Second North
if I'm going to the bookstore,
First North for downtown,
Center for home.
They made it one way last year,
forcing eastbound drivers back
into the parallel streets
where everyone knows.

THE WART DOCTOR MAKES A HOUSE CALL

It started on the right top
of my left second toe, a callus
from rubbing Biggie, I thought at first,
but then Biggie got one too.
Verruca vulgaris grew bigger, harder,
and when one appeared on a third toe,
what had been painless,
not even particularly unsightly,
became fleshy disintegration,
gnashing pain.

Every week they freeze the invaders
with bursts of liquid nitrogen,
create a blister of blood
between wart and underlying tissue, hope
one day to reach an uninfected layer.
A few days of not incidental pain, a week or two
of waiting, then scalpel or eager fingernail
pops the now-dry blister
and voila! One layer gone.

The doctor broke his thumb skiing
so he operates with blade between index and middle,
cleaving bad from good without spilling a drop.
I'm so impressed, I ask him home,
and he takes his blade to my habits,
my marriage, my self-esteem,
til all that's left is right,
half-bodies trying fruitlessly to mate,
half-mind hopelessly made up.

Marty Nyikos

Uncle Bela

Uncle Bela sits on a stump, his pocket knife expertly carving a thick slab of
bacon.
One eye, not wanting to give up his secrets, sightless,
The other, he says, able to see a coin from a thousand meters.
Sadly, it sees only the past. Remembering attributes an eagle would envy.
His gnarled hands hold the knife between tree root fingers,
Scarred from molding steel into locks.
He made puppets for the children.
Hoping to keep them from knowing the horrors of where they were.
Their parents, only paying him in knowing glances, bowed heads. Promises.

Bela looks at me, his mouth turns to a smile. A gate coming off its hinges.
*"Csak egyel, fiam."** He tells me, his large hand on my back, smile never wavering.

I'll never know what he has gone through.
He doesn't talk of his medals my mother will later give me for my birthday.
I take the bread, now saturated with the grease off the dripping bacon.
Take a bite and savor the flavor.
No, the time.

*"Just eat, my son."

Zombie Proof Fence

When other kids were making tree houses,
I built a zombie proof fence.
My friends helped, naturally,
They knew the danger we were in.

We built the fence out of wood,
But if the infection lasted a while,
We would need to build a permanent one,
Brick would probably be best.

Not a night could go by
But we too started to hear them.
It was a good thing we got our dad

To install the spotlight.
For our double A's kept running out.

The fence wasn't very high,
Bu then it didn't need to be.
For everyone knows
That zombies can't jump.

We were even going to build a moat,
But when our hands started to hurt,
And the lemonade stopped flowing,
We quickly decided against it.

Now we wait,
Huddled together anxiously
Ready for anything,
Listening to their moans
Just beyond my zombie proof fence.

My Manticore

My manticore sleeps
Camouflaged on a pillow.
His ancient bones stick
Out from under his skin.

His terrorizing days
Are long since forgotten.
His melodious song, barely heard.

"I like his square face,"
The comment is made.
After all, she should know.

He can't sit down all the way.
And his legs are crooked.
But he still manages somehow.

My manticore looks up,
As if he knows we are talking
About him.

His face is more feline than human.
His teeth, all three sets, are worn,

His tail's spines are worthless,
But they are worth something to me.
I've collected them all.

His mane has fallen out
And blown away.
He hasn't even noticed.

He is content
To sit in my lap.
"This is the happiest he's been."
At least I can give him that.

I scratch under his chin
And he moves weakly toward me
As if only remembering how to respond.

I have to go now,
But I'll know
I can always find him when I come home.

Heather Frost

THE TRUEST CHARACTER

James Ben Fabbit—pen name J. B. Fabbit—stared at the blinking curser on the screen, a hypnotic throb that only enhanced the steady pounding in his temporal lobe. He re-read the last few lines he'd written, hoping *this* time he'd find fresh inspiration.

"What are these things?" Jenna's voice wavered, and the beam of her flashlight sliced over the gray-skinned bodies laid out in rows upon the warehouse floor.

Steven swallowed hard, his own flashlight steady as he focused on the nearest inert form at his feet. "Evidence. Evidence of the biggest conspiracy yet. They're aliens, Jenna. And the government knew all along."

Just then the overhead lights hummed to life, and a deep, smooth voice settled over them, coming from the metal walkway above them. "Yes. And now you will both pay the price of your curiosity."

It was Mr. Roth.

Fabbit scowled. The words were as flat as his characters, style, plot, and tone. Flat; all flat. This was supposed to be his masterpiece, and yet he found himself reduced to useless stereotypes, over-the-top dramatics, and over-done plot lines. It was enough to make him re-think his life's ambition to become a novelist, and it certainly did nothing for his headache.

He huffed loudly in the sparse apartment, shoving back from his desk. In the medicine cabinet he found the nearly empty bottle of Tylenol and popped two tablets into his mouth. He hadn't shaved in over a week and the stubble was beginning to itch. His gray eyes were bloodshot; he leaned closer to the mirror and examined the lines on his long face. Neal Stubbs, his old college roommate and best friend, certainly didn't look as worn down, though they were both barely thirty.

He replaced the medication in the cupboard, just as his cell phone buzzed in his pocket. He drew it out, glad for the distraction.

"Hey Mom."

"James, how's the novel coming?"

She was easily his biggest fan; she actually read what he wrote. "Kind of slow today, actually."

"Oh no, I'm sorry to hear that. I want to find out what happens to Jenna and Steven. You know you left me hanging, right? They were about to sneak into the warehouse."

A smile tugged at his lips. "I know. I'm sorry."

"Sometimes I don't think you are. You're smiling right now, aren't you?"

"Guilty."

"Well, stop that obnoxious smiling and start writing!"

Fabbit wandered back into his dual kitchen and office, phone at his ear. "Easier said than done."

"Well, you said I could pester you any time about it. You asked me too, actually."

"Right. Well, I don't know that I'm going to get any more writing done today..."

"Uh-uh. I knew there was a reason I called you when I did. You were about to quit for the day, weren't you? James, you've been working on that chapter for days!"

"I know."

"You need to shut out the inner critic you're always talking about and just write."

"But it's crap."

"No, it's not."

"You have to say that, Mom."

"You mean because I have impeccable honesty?"

He grinned. "Because you're my mother. And I don't know how much I can trust you, since you still have my second-grade poem framed in the living room."

"It won first place!"

"In second grade."

"It still won. Now. Back to your computer, young man, and do something productive."

Fabbit sighed, but smiled. "Thanks, Mom."

"Of course. Now go! And if Jenna dies, I'll kill you."

He chuckled at the old threat, even as he hung up. Honestly, Jenna might die before the end. He hadn't decided. It depended on how much trouble she gave him in the chapters ahead. He felt a little evil when he thought about it like that, but one of his professors in college had told him that writers had to be a little bit evil sometimes.

Fabbit stood behind his chair, facing his laptop. He didn't sit as he stared at the laptop's screen, fingers tapping against his legs. He read through the familiar words once more. They only managed to feel drier than before.

Well, he wouldn't get any writing done with that chapter, regardless of his mother's wishes, at least until his headache dissolved. He'd give himself a short break from the agony of writers block, but still be productive.

Sinking into the chair, he settled his fingers over the keyboard and typed a plea to Google: *How do I make my pathetic characters cooperate?*

His skimmed the top results before settling on the title of a blog post: The Truest Character.

The post was quite short, and didn't exactly reveal anything new. Yes, his story needed real characters, and of course having strong characters would make the writing process easier. He was nearly ready to leave the blog behind, but his eyes lingered over a passage.

Begin with your villain. Explore their motivations. Thoreau said, "Dreams are the touchstones of our characters." That certainly applies to villains as well. So take your villain, and just write about him: describe his bedroom, his space. Write scenes that transpired when the villain was a child, an adolescent, an adult—fears and dreams; likes and dislikes; memories and nightmares. Learn everything you can. This is the key to unlocking the entire story. As John Rogers said, "You don't really understand an antagonist until you understand why he's a protagonist in his own version of the world."

Both intrigued and frustrated by the simple "answer" to his writers block, Fabbit scrolled through the pages and pages of comments. Most praised the blog writer and agreed amongst themselves that her methods had worked for them. One specifically drew his eye:

Iwant2believe93 says: This is amazing! It totally worked for me, and I've never felt more free.

If there was anything Fabbit wanted, it was freedom from writers block. And at this point, he was willing to try just about anything, even the obvious.

Considering his own villain, the mysterious and betraying Mr. Roth, Fabbit found that—once again—he'd relied on clichés. Roth had a nervous tick: his eye twitched. He had an estranged daughter, age twelve. Roth was in his later forties, graying hair, an FBI special agent thought at first to be a friend, then a representation of corrupt government. Not exactly the deepest character.

Fabbit glanced around his bachelor apartment, noting the breakfast dishes in the sink. Roth probably did his dishes the moment he got them dirty. He was meticulous that way. He spotted the calendar on the wall. Tropical birds. No way Roth would like that. He was more of a sunset kind of person.

Fabbit had enough to get started. He pulled up a fresh document and began to describe Roth's apartment, noting the dishes tidbit, and the calendar, then he started listing the CDs lining Roth's bookshelf, all of them from popular 80s bands.

* * *

"Who can it be knocking at my door?/Go 'way, don't come 'round here no more/Can't you see that it's late at night?/I'm very tired and I'm not feeling right ..."

Fabbit blinked at the computer screen, the music almost managing to drown out the incessant buzzing of his cell phone. It wouldn't be his mother. He'd talked to her the other day and begged her to stop calling for a while. No, everything was fine, but he was making progress and he didn't want to be disturbed when he was in the zone. Yes, he'd call her later.

He hadn't, though.

He was making headway on deepening Mr. Roth's character, though. He'd immersed himself in the personality completely. He'd been listening to *Queen* and *The Police* and *Men At Work* almost nonstop, since they were Roth's favorites. He had also learned that Mr. Roth hated sausage, and enjoyed reading Edgar Allen Poe.

Fabbit realized distantly that the phone had gone silent.

He was currently working on a scene that took place early on in the novel. Revising the conversation between Mr. Roth and Steven, the main character, was exciting, since Fabbit was now open to so many new possibilities.

"Why are you doing this?" Steven asked.

Mr. Roth's eye twitched, his smile unwavering across the table. "I'm willing to help you, Steven. And Jenna, of course."

"What you're trying to do isn't right. It's not fair."

"You believe our current position is fair?"

"I won't help you."

Mr. Roth straightened. "Very well. It seemed only right that I offered you and Jenna the chance to get out of this."

There was a hard knock on the front door. Fabbit's fingers hung over the keys, suspended, unsure.

He'd lost his train of thought.

"I can hear the music," a voice called through the front door. "I know you're home!"

Fabbit sighed and pushed back from his desk. He opened the door and found Neal Stubbs standing there with a pizza box.

"I've been calling you all day," Stubbs complained.

"Sorry, I've been busy."

Stubbs stepped into the apartment and Fabbit closed the door. By the time he turned, Stubbs was already in the kitchen, plopping the pizza on the counter. He lifted a slim book and eyed it doubtfully. "Edgar Allen Poe? I didn't know you liked horror."

"I didn't know you knew Poe."

"Even illiterates know the freakiness of Poe." Stubbs flipped open to the bookmarked short story, Roth's favorite: *Ligeia*.

"What are you doing here?" Fabbit asked, knowing he sounded too impatient.

Stubbs dropped the book and grinned. "I got it, man. I got the promotion!"

"Really? That's ... great."

"It's more than great." Stubbs caught sight of the glowing laptop. "How's the bestseller coming?"

Fabbit couldn't stop the smile that broke free. "Fabulously."

"You hungry?"

Now that he could smell the pizza, he realized he was ravenous. When had he last eaten? He instinctively checked the sink to count the dishes, but it was empty.

"You know it's July, right?"

"Huh?"

Stubbs gestured with his chin at the calendar on the wall, which showed June's Moluccan Cockatoo.

Fabbit frowned. "Yeah. Just barely, though." He moved to change the month while Stubbs searched out a couple of plates. He pulled the calendar down and Stubbs asked about drinks, so Fabbit set the calendar on the counter. He could hang it again after they ate.

"So," Stubbs said a little later, reclining on the couch. "You're saying that whoever wrote that post is saving your soul or something?"

"Not my soul," Fabbit disagreed, plucking the sausage off his three meat pizza. "*Roth's* soul. The whole soul of the book, really. It's amazing. I'm learning things about Roth I never knew, and it's opening so many doors for the entire plot! I actually think I'm going to make Roth my protagonist."

"Don't you need a bad guy, though?"

"Sure—that's what Steven and Jenna are for, now." His mom would hate that, but he had to write what his characters wanted. That's just how writing was.

Stubbs shook his head. "If you say so." He frowned slightly. "You just need to make sure you don't stay in this apartment so much. It can't be good for you. I think I see some gray hairs ..."

* * *

It was 3:34am, six weeks since he'd read the blog post. At least, he thought that's how long it had been; he hadn't bothered to rehang that calendar, so he wasn't sure.

Fabbit was close to finishing his novel. He hadn't left his apartment in days. The intense drive to finish the book was keeping him from eating, sleeping— his phone had died a couple days ago, and he couldn't be bothered to find the charger. His limbs felt heavy, but his mind was achingly alert. He wrote constantly. His fingers cramped, but he forced himself to keep going. Even when he typed words wrong, he kept going. He knew he needed a break—he'd even typed *Fabbit* instead of *Roth* several times, but he'd simply frowned, hit backspace six times, then started again.

His eyelid trembled in a drawn out twitch. Sweat beaded at his hairline as he stared at the moving cursor. He was writing a conversation between Steven, Jenna, and Mr. Roth, but the words weren't making much sense. Still, Fabbit typed—intrigued by the fluidity of the words coming to mind.

Steven and Jenna were tied to the hard-backed chairs, their eyes wide at the revelations being told to them.

Fabbit frowned. What revelations? The alien discovery? That must be it ... But hadn't he already written that scene?

Mr. Roth skimmed his fingers over the gray streaks at his temples, his tone regretful as he paced the cold concrete floor. "You really shouldn't have tried to interfere."

Steven grunted, straining against the rope.

"You can't do this!" Jenna cried. "Fabbit doesn't know what he's doing!"

Fabbit blinked, staring at his own name. His finger twitched toward the backspace key, but he didn't hit it. He just continued writing the scene, as if his name was supposed to be in there. Somehow, he knew it was *supposed* to be there. He winced at the sudden pressure in his head, his hands dancing over the keyboard.

"Stop writing!" Steven shouted. "You need to stop right now!"

Fabbit's mouth went dry. This wasn't right. His fingers were rigid, unstoppable.

Mr. Roth grinned. "It's too late for that. In fact, there's really not much time left for anything. I've got places to be." He reached into his suit, drawing out a handgun.

Fabbit felt sweat rolling down the side of his face. His heart pounded. He typed haltingly, but he couldn't stop, even though he wanted to.

Did he want to?

He wasn't sure anymore.

But the curser pushed forward, even as he stared at his fingers. His eyes lifted and he skimmed over the words he'd missed.

Steven was trying to jerk out of his bindings, rocking the chair with his efforts. "You can't do this, Roth. You're not meant to do this."

"Fabbit!" Jenna screamed, eyes widening as Roth cocked his weapon. "Delete this now! He's in your head! Delete the whole thing, right now!"

Fabbit flinched. He tried to clench his hands to fists, tried to pull away from the laptop, but he couldn't. He gulped as the words rushed on.

Mr. Roth leveled the gun at Jenna's chest and squeezed off a round. She cried out and slumped forward, breath stuttering out.

Fabbit gasped, a strangled sound. Blood roared in his ears. His head was groaning with pain. His vision sparked, and then he wasn't staring at the computer screen. He was staring at Steven, and Steven was staring at him. Fabbit could feel the weight of the gun in his hand as he levelled it at Steven. No. *No!*

Jenna was dead.

The gun fired again and Steven sagged against the chair, also dead.

Fabbit yelled and dropped the gun. Even as it clattered to the floor, he knew he hadn't dropped it voluntarily. Something had made him drop it. Fabbit curled his fingers in his hair, breathing raggedly.

A shadowy figure rippled at the edge of vision. Fabbit spun to face it.

Roth.

Roth grinned, his body mostly transparent. Still, he managed to stoop and lift the gun.

Fabbit's head throbbed and he fell to his knees. "What's going on?" he choked. "Who's writing this?"

Mr. Roth lifted an eyebrow. "I thought that was obvious?" He raised the gun, aiming it at Fabbit's head.

The bullet discharged and Fabbit's body crumpled to the floor.

Mr. Roth was free.

Roth leaned back after typing the final words, flexing his tight fingers. He felt his lips relax in an easy smile as he glanced around the sparse apartment. He would need to get a bookshelf or two, but that could wait until tomorrow. Other than that, Fabbit had prepared things quite nicely.

Roth opened a browser and clicked through the search history, finding the blog post. He scrolled down to the comments and quickly inserted his own.

j.b.fabbit says: Agreed! This exercise is incredible. Count me as another success.

SLAM POETRY AND FLASH PROSE

Featuring
Performance Artist Darren Edwards
and the
Utah State University Bull Pen Creative Writing Club

Darren Edwards

Privilege

Noun: a special right, advantage, or immunity granted or available only to a particular person or group of people.

As in, the last time I spoke at Utah State University, I had the privilege of not worrying that someone might attack me with "Assault rifles, multiple pistols and a collection of pipe bombs" which they have "at [their] disposal."

I have the privilege of living in a system that isn't pockmarked with loopholes legalizing prejudice against me, where I can walk away from a police officer, play my music loud, and eat skittles without the fear of being fatally shot.

I have the privilege of society understanding and accepting my sexuality and gender without question, of never having to hear my parents identify me by anything other than what I am, or fearing that my father may stab me to death because I'm trying to feel more comfortable in my own skin.

Walking into a job interview, I have worried that they might not like my flip-flops and a neck tie combo, but never has the concern that my heritage could cost me the job or the amount of cleavage I show override my personal merit entered into the equation.

You see, I am the privileged of the privileged. I'm not saying that I haven't earned what I have, but I am fortunate that this misconception is my biggest fear when society dissects my lineage, sexuality, and gender—you know, rather than lynch mobs, sexual harassment, and systematic discrimination.

I am not responsible for the sins of my forefathers, and I am not accountable for the hate and prejudice slung about by other white men, but I do sit in a seat of privilege created by a history infused, inseparably, with these things.

Privilege might be a noun, but it's not something I can own. No matter how hard I try, I'll never be fully aware of the struggles the color of my skin and my possession of a penis exempt me from. And saying that I can or do is just a cover story for throwing in the towel because their pain is too uncomfortable for me to think about.

Thank god, privilege isn't just a noun.

Privilege
Verb: grant a privilege or privileges to.

Because I live in a society where, however unjustly, my voice is often heard above the cries of others.

Because I'm assured more safety, a bigger platform, and a fraction of the road-blocks so many others face, may god grant me the intelligence to turn my priv-ileges into action, to work toward a day when women like Anita Sarkeesian can speak their mind without a shit storm of death threats, where names like Walter Scott, Jordan Davis, and Trevon Martin are attached to their accomplishments not obituaries, where the life stories of Leelah Alcorn and Bri Golec don't end in tragedy but go on in a beautiful exploration of self.

And bless that I can do this while avoiding some fucked up savior complex, because they don't need my white male greatness to pull them up.

What we need is for all of us to tear this system down.

HEMATOLOGY

Since Anthony van Leeuwenhoek
invented the microscope in 1642,
we've mapped the circulation of blood,
identified individual blood types,
ended the practice of bloodletting as
a cure for disease
and subdivided blood into its base
components.
Each transparent red bead spread between
glass slides, teaching us that much
more about ourselves.

> Jacobus de Voragine's *Golden Legend*
> is full of people who crawled toward death
> begging to become martyrs:

Dreaming of a heavenly throne, Saint Longinus ordered his own
beheading
and Saint Boniface was "eager" to have splinters driven under his finger
nails, have his flesh torn
by metal hooks, and to eventually be dipped head first in a tub of boiling
pitch.

It's been hundreds of years since
we believed it was our lungs
not our hearts that give the gentle
flex and tremble that cause blood to move.

In the beginning of the second century
Roman authorities publicly tortured
and executed
Rabbi 'Aqibha ben Yoseph
to destroy the spirit of his people

Falsely imprisoned
in Carthage Illinois,
Joseph Smith rushed
the mob of gunmen
as they came through the door

Tied to a tree,
Saint Sebastian's heart was pierced
by an arrow,
and Diocletian commanded his men
to keep firing

until the snap of bow strings filled the air
and Sebastian's chest couldn't be seen
for the quills.

The average life span of a red blood cell is
only 120 days long, but our bone marrow
is constantly replacing them as they expire,
each cell birthed from a dizzying
circle of transformations,
evolutions,
birth after birth
from stem cell
to erythrocyte.

John Huss kept his silence
as they led him to the stake
for refusing to recant his beliefs
and acknowledge the papal position
as divinely ordained

Between 3 and 5 thousand people were killed
during the 140 years of the Spanish Inquisition

Faith, it would appear,
runs in our blood
because too often
spilling one,
is the most effective way
we know to show
the others
existence.

Yet, in the 300 plus years
since Leeuwenhoek
first looked at the gently dipping ovals
that rush through us,
 a gallon and a half at once,
we've found nothing
to substantiate this belief.

Still, we spill more blood,
red pools diffusing light,
baptizing sod and stone
in this faith.

We spill more blood,
and when the gallons
are gone,
when humanities veins have thinned past transparency
when its marrow has dried and dusted,
is there a lesson that echoes
from the hollow bones?
Does it matter what hymn is created
with this final collapse
if there is no one left to sing it?

Alex Bullock

THE WAVES

When I was little,
I went to my mother's dinner parties a godless child.
I had scraped knees, missing teeth, and untamed hair
scarcely masked by the patterns of pretty dresses.
The other ladies would always say,
"She's going to be so beautiful someday."
Then, their words meant nothing to me.
They were strong ocean waves
but I was far away,
deep in brine,
chasing whales and shipwrecks.

But a few years later found me hugging the toilet
in pursuit of the 'Beauty' that had eluded me.
I couldn't find Her in the mirror
and for some damn reason I thought She was in the toilet,
and in restraint,
and in "No, I already ate."

I couldn't realize that
She was never in the bathroom to begin with.

I found Her when I was covered in salt.
Not only when I was a little girl with an outlandish imagination,
but when I set my feelings free
and gave salty goodbye kisses
wet with tears that couldn't really decide if they were happy or sad
or nervous.

I found beauty when I talked to my other feelings too.
They became my guardian angels,
my trusty compass that may not always point north
but kept pulling me to new horizons.
My emotions and I were soon good friends,
all of them,
the good and bad.
Because they always had new things to tell me
like when they told me to let go of the boy
who said he would always keep me safe.

Or when they quietly reminded me that
I could still forgive those closest to me,
and that maybe I was the one who needed forgiveness.

I found people who understood my feelings.
I gave them my heart and in turn they gave me their hands,
to hold,
or to lift me up,
or just to rest lightly on my shoulder
as a gentle reminder that I don't have to be alone.

Around this time, I found my vertebrae,
and they were just as strong as those bones of the shipwrecks
I once played in,
the ones that the life had long left
but the frames were sturdy as ever.
I stood up as tall as I could,
I thought my eyes would touch the big dipper,
and I remembered what to say to boys
who had lost their compasses,
and got the wrong and right directions all jumbled together.

I've been waking up in nests and unfolding myself like flower petals.
The sun smiles at me and I can't help but hum like a fat bumblebee,
grateful for breakfasts of juicy blackberries and meditation.
I've been feeling like I'm on the edge of something huge
and everything in the world is surging past me,
pushing me,
telling me that I'm so close
so close.

It was the waves that had been drowning me,
not the strong currents beyond the shallow water.
The surface could only reflect back at the surface.
It neglected to tell me that my skinned knees told their own stories,
that my blood and bones wanted adventure
and even after wrong turns that proved I could still fall down
they would do absolutely everything, with every cell available,
to push out the hurt and dirt that seeped in through my skin,
to scab over and to make me whole again.

I found myself returning to the bathroom,
but I made sure I looked for myself in mirrors,
not expectations.
I took care of the body that was working so hard to take care of me.

The world has turned from trivial waves crashing
to whale song.
To a humming of bees,
whistling mountain winds, and murmuring deep-sea currents.
The world is full of spirit, and laughter.
I've finally found Beauty, and I've been calling her the wrong name all along.
Her name is love.

Brittney McDonald

JUMP

You stand at the bottom of our stairs,
Knee cocked and eager
As you stretch your legs,
Prepare to jump up five steps at a time,
Look for my eyes across the room
To show me that you can make it.

I watch you from the couch
That in Summer swallowed us whole,
Sucked sweat from our bones
As suns sank behind mountains
And the TV lured us into the dark
That made you Man, and me Yours.

After months of hours that turned
Into days between our sweating hands
Winter came: You hung blue curtains
And it was dark all days.
We cut ourselves on razor-laced thongs
And experimented with
"I'm sorry"—
Meaning:
Nothing has loved me better
And my feet poke out naked at night
Because you steal red feather blankets
We don't know how to share.

Now it's the Spring that came too soon
And I'm trying to think of light
But there you stand,
Knee cocked.
Even though Summer will be home soon
And I've looked at you for months,
I want to see you take five stairs at once,
Watch you jump.

Millie Tullis

MAD

I close my eyes and
You plant flaking lips on me.
All the world
Should have slowed. But all I wanted
Was for you to
Drop dead.
              I lift my lids
Only to see your rabbit eyes.
And all is born
Within me, without you. It could mean everything
To see how you fear me,
Again, again.

I think I made
You kiss me. I wondered what it would be,
What it would mean, to have
You up inside
Caught in the gleaming hook of my body,
But shut, cleanly out, of my grey matter,
My head.

Jordon Roberts

Take Cymbalta

For five years, I've swallowed a capsule that swallows
my depression. A blue and white gymnast performing a balancing
act. Tiptoeing the thin threads separating
my brain's chemicals. Chemicals like hope and reality
battling for the territories in my mind.
The reality of desiring to slice
my wrists ripping apart the hope
of watching another sunrise into shreds
too small to pick up and piece
back together with false smiles
and the thought that tomorrow
will be better.
Take Cymbalta, the doctor said. Create
a collage of the broken
bits, glue them together
with duloxetine hydrochloride. Take
Cymbalta and view reality through hope stained
glasses.
The fear of testing the waters
of another hour transformed
into swan diving into every second
of breath flooding into my chest.
Isolation turned into breaking
from the bars built
by my own inhibitions. Life
became happy. I became happy.
For five years, I've swallowed a pill that swallows
me. Choking on my ripped fingernails as I crawl
up its throat trying to hold
on to who I am.
Since senior year of high school
my friends, my family stare
into my eyes searching for signs
of depression.
*You seem down today. It looks
like you've been crying. Did you take
your medication?*
I cry when Old Yeller dies. I cry
when my cousin refuses

to eat because she does not feel
beautiful. I cry when I remember
my best friend who hung himself
from a barn rafter because he could not see
the light breaking through the grey and black storm
that is depression.
Cymbalta clutches to my elbow, escorts
me through hallways peeling
away panic attacks, plucking unexplainable
tears from my cheeks, salty diamonds
falling every hour. I'm trapped
under blue and white bricks. Suffocating
within walls weak enough to dissolve
on my tongue, but strong enough I can't break free.
So take Cymbalta.
Take away the fear so crushing it broke
my legs, stopped me from running toward the horizon
and seeing what lies behind it. Stop me
from wearing clothes too big for me because I want to feel
like more of a person. Take away the idea
that I am only sand skin dragging crumbling bones.
But don't take Cymbalta.
Don't take my light, stop bringing back to a pill popper.
Stop dragging me back to someone who can only survive
in the crook of your embrace
while you bury the dusty black and white memories
of who I used to be. Bury them under
I can't get up in the morning without you
and I can't see my friends unless your blood
runs through mine and I won't even try
to go a day without swallowing you.
So take Cymbalta. But don't steal
my chance to live. Don't steal my chance
to be me. Because I am more
than you.

Tessa Nicolaides

Air

My nephew Maxwell runs with his legs pointed in and woodchips spray with each step. If he doesn't keep up his speed, he will topple over. He throws his arms out wide, letting the crisp air coat them. I notice his cheeks are rosy as he tilts his head back to let out a long deep howl. He stops and spins around, laughing harder each time he faces me again, seeing the blurry image of me sitting on the park bench. Then he tumbles over, and as he lies on the ground he lets out one last bursting breath.

I cry. We sit in the waiting room surrounded by dollhouses and fire trucks. A space laced with *Smarties* wrappers, and *Doc Mcstuffins* stickers. And I cry. Because of his form of Leukemia, Steve is the oldest patient at Primary Children's Hospital. He doubles most of the others people in age, and now his body looks even older. Like it decided to try and fill the role of the eldest. My sisters visiting badge says, "parent" under her name because the word "wife" has no purpose here. And after today, the word "wife" could lose its purpose for my sister all-together. I focus on the doors lined with "parent sleeping room," and notice how they all say "in use." I think about the moms and dads that sleep there every night. The people that now consider it home. I wonder if they lay awake staring at the ceilings trying to rub the pain on their children's faces out of their eyes. Or maybe they dream, dream of their kid covered in sand at the park. Or perhaps they cry themselves to sleep, letting their tears coat a familiar pillow. I blink trying to force the tears away hoping to forget how his skin looked like a latex glove squeezing his bones and organs out. Trying to forget how the bleached white hospital sheets had more color than him.

Beep. Steve takes a breath that sounds like air seeping through the crack of a window. Beep. The nurse shoves a long tube down his throat pulling green liquid back up. Beep. I look at my sister as tears settle on the tips of her eyelashes. Beep.

I leave the room and Steve's sister, Lauren, meets me in the hallway. Her pregnant belly gets in the way as we hug, making it so my head crashes into her neck. "I love you like my own family you know that right?" I nod and I notice her tears seeping into my gray sweatshirt. I look at her puffy, blotchy face, and I'm afraid she may burst. I don't know much about her, because we are only related through Steve marrying my sister. But her hug is tight like she meant the comment. *He will live. He will make it.* She doesn't say this to me, but like she's trying to convince herself. Her voice rises, getting higher at the end of the word "live," like she asked a question. She doesn't cry anymore. She talks about her brother, Steve, that survived cancer five years ago, but never got better. Her brother that needs a machine to force his 28-year-old lungs to breathe. Her brother that would leave my 28- year-old sister a widow. Her brother that would drag his oxygen tank up the basement stairs without being asked, to talk to me about my bad day. Her brother whose skin is so tight that it leaves no space for his bones. She talks about her brother, but doesn't cry. I cry.

The sun starts to set over the park and Maxwell runs to me. I pick him up as his chest rises and falls. He laughs delaying each short inhale of air. He focuses on the sun grazing the mountaintops. And his giant golden brown eyes melt into Steve's blue ones. "Just breathe," I whisper into his ear. And I realize in that moment I'm not saying it to him. I think of Steve lying in the same hospital bed that he got put in three days ago. I think of all the people huddled around him. And as Maxwell's breathing slows down, I realize not much separates Max from Steve. Or from me and Steve. Not much separates the living from the dying. Just a few breaths.

Travis C. Williams

CHANGE

I spill my
intestinal response
all over you
in hopes
my guts
help your teeth
dance and
maybe my ink
can be the start of
some optimism.
Like a daily tattooing
of your heart upon
your sleeve
and actually believing it.

I've got little atoms
cold as dippin dots
that chill up inside
caused by a
pitter patter in
the chest that
bleeds into
the stomach
from the drizzlings
of all my wasted saliva.

When my belly gets drenched
I take a drive
to jog on the jaw,
pump
on the gas,
while I
chew on words
with the
windows cracked
lettin that
cranky wind
crackle up
my spine.

Each breath's reminding
Confidence is a lock;
The Key is smiling.

Ignite up those piano teeth
Igniting that spark
Turn on the tunes
Turn over embodiments
Turn on the wheel
and get turnt up so much
yo chest leave yo body
And you feel
light.
Like a feather
that leads magnetized
mesmerized
by the tinglings
in the pinkie
trickling down the feet
back up into
this slobberin pink thing
Saying:

Lips need to be rubbed like matchbooks.
Try to turn down the static knowing the change
in cup holders is meant for our chalices.

Dirty dashboards are full
of filthy feathers
arranged only for your current situation.

Never sure when
how
why
they got there.
Like not quite sure
if I think the same things
as that other tethered dust.

Like the bum's eyes
asking for
different change
than that of his words
or his cup.
Acting

on the
ironic synonymous paradox
that you get what you ask for.

Only a little different.

Jace Smellie

Maradona's Legacy

"See here, Lio will save the day," said a hopeful Charlie pointing toward the flat screen television with his left hand, a flour tortilla chip still pressed between his fingers. "We can always count on Messi." In his right hand he held a blue plastic bowl of guacamole. He stared intently toward the screen. It was the closing minutes of extra time in the 2014 FIFA World Cup. Mario Gotze had just scored the go ahead goal for Germany, and now Lionel Messi was lining up a free kick from well outside the box. Clearly, this was their last chance.

The two-bedroom apartment wasn't clean, but it wasn't filthy either. The living room had a couch and a love seat that didn't match, and a very old oval shaped wooden coffee table sat in the middle of the living room with a thin layer of dust covering the parts that weren't covered by soda cans and bags of chips. Charlie wore his authentic FC Barcelona jersey he had purchased that year online. The back of it read, "MESSI" and "10."

"I don't know man, he's pretty far out there," said Charlie's roommate Johnny as Messi placed the ball down on the spot the referee had designated. "I think he probably ought to just turn it into a cross and try to bend it back for the other—"

"Ah ah ah!" Charlie interrupted sharply, pointing a finger covered in salt toward Johnny sitting on the love seat without taking his eyes off the television. "He'll take the shot; he can make it."

"I wouldn't be so sure."

"No, he can do it!" Charlie was sitting up on the edge of the worn brown polyester couch cushion. He reached beneath his neck and grabbed the collar of his jersey. He pulled it up toward his lips and kissed it softly. "He can do it."

Lionel Messi lined up his shot. He ran up and kicked with his powerful left foot. The ball had a lot of pace on it, but it sailed well over the top of the crossbar—nothing.

Charlie let out an audible growl of agony as he bounced back into the back of the couch and ran both hands through his long dark brown hair.

"Dang," Johnny said casually, "I guess he's just no Maradona."

"OH HELL NO!" Charlie sprung back up in his seat and looked directly at Johnny who sat relaxingly in the big maroon love seat holding a Diet Pepsi in his left hand. "No, don't even go there right now!"

"What?! I thought that's what you said?! He has to win this World Cup to prove himself better than Maradona right?"

"No, he has to prove it to Argentina! Not to us."

"How do we know?! We've never seen Maradona play."

"Diego Maradona is shit. That's how we know! The man is a classless jealous prick. When he was the coach last World Cup he stuck Messi in the midfield trying to keep him at bay. How ironic, the man the entire country praises as a soccer god did all he could when he was in charge of the nation's team to prevent their success. He'd rather have kept Messi at bay and not win the World Cup than allow Messi to shine and bring the cup home for their homeland! Classless!"

Charlie reached to the coffee table and grabbed another chip. "Oh, and not to mention the drugs! *Loads* of drugs! The man is like a walking cocaine farm! Even when he was playing he was getting caught with coke and prostitutes! They say he was even involved with the Italian Mafia when he was playing club ball there."

"That's all just alleged."

"Right, 'allegedly this,' and 'allegedly that.' Argentina would never allow anything negative about their 1986 world cup savior be for certain. Even just casually talking about the possibility would be sacrilege! Ha, it'd be like accusing the Pope himself!"

"Have you ever been to Argentina?" Johnny asked abruptly.

"What?" Charlie asked after a brief pause to look at the game. The referee blew his whistle for the end of extra time. The game was over.

"You've never been to Argentina right? And I'd almost bet you've never even met an actual Argentine, right?"

Charlie stammered, "Well, I mean, I guess...I probably have once, I don't know, it doesn't matter though, everyone knows—"

"Everyone knows that all Argentines are oblivious to Maradona's imperfections? That all Argentines don't respect Messi because he still hasn't won a world cup? That Messi is the best player ever in the world?" Johnny paused briefly. Charlie gave no response, but just stared stunned at Johnny. "I mean, who cares right? If Messi is the best in the world, that's cool; he's not the only one who decides if Argentina wins a world cup though! You saw Higuain shank the best look of the game in the first half! So what good is it focusing on all that?"

After some slight hesitation, "It's like I said, Messi needs to prove—"

"He doesn't need to prove shit!" The television screen zoomed in on a group of drunk German fans waving a giant flag of red, yellow, and black. Johnny continued, "It's the 21st Century right? They've got cable in Argentina—they've got the internet! It's no mystery what Lio's been doing over in Barcelona. He is the best, I'll buy that, but winning a world cup doesn't mean a thing if you ask me. But I'm no Argentine."

They continued to watch up until Lionel Messi was presented with the golden boot award, but then they turned the TV off when they got ready to present the German national team with the cup. Charlie went back into his room and hung up his jersey, while Johnny cleaned off the coffee table.

Alyssa Quinn

Mormon Kids

On Saturday night, her fingers dip blue dye
onto long yellow locks. The bathroom tile
smudges indigo,
and soap bars slip from
stained palms.
The next day, on the phone, she tells her mom.
"It's just a little bit of blue. Mom? Mom, are you crying?
Gosh Mom, it's only hair! *Mom, why are you crying?*"

We
are a generation of children
who have disappointed our mothers.
We have sling-shot
as far from our past as possible,
but every time we call home,
there it is, hissing over the wires.

We toss back black coffee, just because we can.
We punch silver studs into tongues,
ink Ginsberg up our ankles,
glut ourselves on
poetry and philosophy.
Outside college classrooms, we share stories of stiff
church pews, of white-bread lies shoved down our throats
for too many years!

We're not angry at God!
We're angry at all the people
who wrapped God up in pretty ribbon
and gave him to us on our birthdays!
We're angry at the people who nailed God
above our beds in cheap gold frames
and commanded us to love him!

But...we can't really be angry at them,
either.
Because the woman who
tugged our hair into too-tight braids every Sunday
is the same woman who nursed us at her
breast.

And the man who dunked us in warm chlorine
at age 8, is the same man
who taught us how to swing a bat,
under the oak trees in the park.

We can't be angry at them.
So we are angry at ourselves,
though we would never
say it out loud.

"Why are you crying, Mom?

Mom, please stop
crying."

Bibleland

The Mary Magdalene scene is performed at eleven, and again at four-thirty. Schedule subject to change in adverse weather conditions. Tickets non-refundable. Apparently resurrections don't happen in the rain.

For the performance, I sport silky blue robes and a long white head cover, a basket full of plastic spices dangling on my arm. When the angel appears, the fog machines spew and the stage lights swivel a blinding white. Yay for special effects.

Jesus arrives wearing a loincloth and a scarlet sash. He used to wear full-length robes, but that was before the new CEO of Bibleland decided the performance was lacking in sexual "umph" and ordered a reinterpretation of the scene. Hence, my deeply plunging neckline and Jesus's Tarzan get-up. I blushed crimson when my parents, fire-and-brimstone evangelicals, attended the performance, but they didn't seem to mind. Dad even let rip a resounding "Hallelujah!" at the end. Embarrassing, but I'll admit--I played up my Christian background when applying for this job. Painted myself as a crucifix-wearing, bible-banging churchgoer. Ha. Haha.

I throw myself at Jesus's sandals, produce what could pass for tears; he lifts me up, pectorals gleaming in the Orlando sun, utters his final line ("Be thou not afraid, for I am risen!"). Trumpets jangle from the speaker system, a trio of fireworks shoots overhead, and we withdraw behind the Styrofoam stone at the entrance to the tomb.

Once we're inside the tomb, which is dark and smells of rubber cement, Jesus slaps my butt. I roll my eyes and disentangle myself from him—no time for games. Not today.

I emerge onto Bibleland's reddish dirt streets, hurry past the low, stone buildings covered in synthetic grapevines. Lines of sunburnt tourists coil around the vendors, buying ice cream cones and plastic crucifix keychains.

Just past the Red Sea Rollercoaster and the Noah's Ark exhibit is Daniel's Lion Enclosure. Two tawny cats prowl beyond the steel grid lines of the cage, shoulder blades rolling with each step. There's the tinny blast of trumpets again, and Daniel appears at the cage entrance, dressed all in leather and bronze. The lions bare their fat, yellow fangs, pull back their thick, tar-black lips, and roar. Daniel enters.

It's all a sham, I know that. Trained to put on a good show, these lions—cleverly named Sodom and Gomorrah— clap their massive paws around Daniels head, then let him wrestle them to the ground, where they emit feeble whines of defeat. Fake, like everything else.

Daniel brandishes a bulky fist in the air. The crowd goes crazy.

It's sickening. While the tourists flock to Daniel for pictures and autographs, I duck around to the lions' indoor enclosure, pulling a ring of keys from the blue folds of my robe.

Inside, Sodom and Gomorrah are sprawled across the cement floor of their cage, gnawing on frozen slabs of pseudo-steak.

"Not like the real thing, is it boys?" I ask. From the ring in my hand, I select a single key and insert it into the padlock on the gate. Two pairs of unblinking eyes look up from their dinners. The gate swings open.

Back outside, the crowd is still thick. Daniel is posing next to a gaggle of prepubescent girls, flexing his biceps for the camera.

"You're late," growls John the Baptist as I sidle up to the churro booth.

"Sorry," I say. "Had something to take care of." From behind the cash register, I have a perfect view. My heart races—any minute now.

"Hey."

I turn around. It's Daniel.

"Oh, hey," I say. "Nice show."

He smirks. "I am merely a vessel for the power of the Lord," he declares. So smug. *So screwed.*

A shriek erupts beyond the lion enclosure. We turn in time to see Sodom and Gomorrah emerging, muzzles pink with blood from their recent meal. More screams. People scatter, dropping popsicles and diet colas in their haste.

A roar rips the air. I turn to Daniel in mock fear.

"Daniel—do something!"

"I—I can't—"

"What do you mean? You're Daniel of the Fucking Lion's Den!"

He just stands there, gaping, as one of the beasts disembowels a hamburger stand. Down the street, screaming guests clog the turnstiles at Bibleland's exit.

I grin.

Oh ye of little faith, I think to myself.

Jeannie Woller

JUST A FEW CONCERNS

Who's to say when I pray
The sound delay from my voice to the sky
Is point five seconds?

It isn't.
It's instant.

But sometimes I'm put on hold.
Waiting.
As the elevator music swirling around in my ears
Is nothing but the same insecurities that made me fall
To my knees
And ask a man to forgive me.

The feminist in me wants to pull out my pepper spray
And say
Stay the hell away from me.

But I don't.
I just squint tighter
And tell my friends I stopped praying years ago.

Maybe prayer's a placebo.
A cube of sugar I swallow
Two to three times a week
Handed to me by a man in white scrubs
Who has yet to scrub the blood
From the holes
In his hands
As he reaches for a soul that may have already
Been lost.

It's no question that I question
His motives.
Because whose blood is on his hands?
His own?
Or the millions of people who,
Dying,
Cry out his name?

ABOUT THE AUTHORS

Shanan Ballam teaches poetry writing, fiction writing, and composition at Utah State University. She is the author of the poetry chapbook *The Red Riding Hood Papers* (Finishing Line 2010) and the full-length poetry collection *Pretty Marrow* (Negative Capability 2013). She is a member of the Utah Arts Council Board of Directors.

Russ Beck received the Frederick Manfred Award for creative writing from the Western Literature Association. He edits and contributes to both *howsmallatrout.wordpress.com* and *braidedbrook.com*. His essays have appeared in *Eat Sleep Fish* and *The Huffington Post*. His first book is a collection of essays he co-wrote called *On Fly-Fishing the Northern Rockies: Essays and Dubious Advice.*

Alex Bullock currently studies English with an emphasis in Creative Writing at Utah State University. She has cycled through various second majors and minors, and has finally settled on studying Philosophy but is still unsure if she will major or minor in it. She loves anything to do with literature, history, astronomy, physics, nature, and art. She spends most of her free time writing, running, and taking care of her houseplants.

Rob Carney is the author of four books and three chapbooks of poems, most recently 88 Maps (Lost Horse Press 2015). He won the 4th Annual *terrain.org* Poetry Prize in 2013 and the Robinson Jeffers/Tor House Foundation Award for Poetry in 2014. His work has appeared in *Cave Wall*, *Mid-American Review*, *saltfront*, *Sugar House Review*, and dozens of other journals, as well as the anthology *Flash Fiction Forward* (W.W. Norton 2006). He is a Professor of English at Utah Valley University and lives in Salt Lake City.

Christopher Cokinos is the author of three books of literary nonfiction, including, most recently, the lyric essay collection *Bodies, of the Holocene*. The winner of a Whiting Award, among other prizes, he has had prose and poetry in such venues as *Poetry*, *TYPO*, *Pank*, *New Delta Review*, *Salon*, *Orion*, *Ecotone*, *Science* and *Extrapolation*. A current manuscript, *The Underneath*, was a recent semi-finalist for the Vassar Miller Prize.

Katharine Coles' sixth collection of poetry, *Flight*, was published in 2016 by Red Hen Press. Her fifth poetry collection, *The Earth Is Not Flat* (Red Hen 2013), was written under the auspices of the U.S. National Science Foundation's Antarctic Artists and Writers Program. Ten poems from that book, translated into German by Klaus Martens, appeared in the summer 2014 issue of the journal *Matrix*; she has also been translated into Spanish, Italian, and Dutch. Her chapbook, *Bewilder*, was published in 2015 by the International Poetry Studies Institute at the University of Canberra. She is also the co-PI on the Poemage project, which develops software for analyzing and visualizing sonic relationships in poetry; she has written a number of scholarly articles and presentations based on this work. A professor at the University of Utah, she served from 2006 to 2012 as Utah Poet Laureate and in 2009 and 2010 as the inaugural director of the Poetry Foundation's Harriet Monroe Poetry Institute. She has received grants and awards from the National Endowment for the Arts, the National Endowment for the Humanities, and the Guggenheim Foundation.

Star Coulbrooke, Poet Laureate of Logan City Utah, is co-founder and coordinator of Helicon West and of Poetry at Three, a longstanding local writing group. Her poems are published nationally in literary journals, magazines, and anthologies. She co-authored a chapbook, *Logan Canyon Blend* (Blue Scarab Press, 2003), with Kenneth W. Brewer, the late former poet laureate of Utah. Her chapbook, *Walking the Bear* (Outlaw Artists Press 2011), is a tribute to the Bear River. Star teaches poetry writing and directs the Utah State University Writing Center.

Brock Dethier spent his misguided youth trying to write fiction but turned to poetry in his 40s when he realized he didn't really care about plot and character development. He published a chapbook of poems, *Ancestor Worship*, in 2007, and a full-length book of poems, *Reclamation*, in 2015. At Utah State University, he tries to supervise the teachers of English 1010 and 2010 and occasionally teaches poetry writing. He has written five books for college composition teachers and students.

Cat Dixon is the author of Eva (Stephen F. Austin University Press, forthcoming 2016), *Our End Has Brought the Spring* (Finishing Line Press, 2015) and *Too Heavy to Carry* (Stephen F. Austin University Press, 2014). She is the managing editor of The Backwaters Press, a nonprofit press in Omaha. She teaches creative writing at the University of Nebraska. Her poetry and reviews have appeared in numerous journals and anthologies including *Sugar House Review, Midwest Quarterly Review, Eclectica*, and *Mid-American Review*. Her website is *catdix.com*.

Darren M. Edwards is a writer. Sometimes he writes poems. Sometimes he writes prose. Sometimes he just writes strings of obscenities. Darren spent two years serving as the Slam Master for Southern Utah, during which time he was also a member of two national poetry slam teams. He has a dog and a wife. She has a small creature growing inside her. In the real world of bills and money, Darren works as the managing editor for the Southern Utah publication, *The Independent*.

Heather Frost has lived in Utah all her life and is hopelessly in love with stories. She is the author of the YA *Seers* trilogy--books two and three were Whitney Award finalists--and also published *Asides*, a collection of short stories. Heather earned her Bachelor's in English with a minor in Folklore at Utah State University. She enjoys reading, writing, cooking, and spending time with her family. By day she works at The Family Place, a non-profit that supports local families, and by night she works on her latest novel. To learn more or contact Heather, visit *HeatherFrost.com*.

Siân Griffiths lives in Ogden, Utah, where she directs the Creative Writing Program at Weber State University. Her work has appeared in *The Georgia Review*, *Fifth Wednesday Journal*, *Quarterly West*, *Ninth Letter*, and *The Rumpus*, among other publications. Her debut novel, *Borrowed Horses* (New Rivers Press), was a semi-finalist for the 2014 VCU Cabell First Novelist Award. For more information, please visit *sbgriffiths.com*.

Ben Gunsberg is a professor of English at Utah State University. His poetry appears in *CutBank*, *The Southeast Review*, and *The South Carolina Review*, among other magazines. He is the author of the chapbook *Rhapsodies with Portraits* (Finishing Line Press, 2015). His poetry manuscript, *Cut Time*, won the University of Michigan's Hopwood Award for Poetry Writing. He lives in Logan, Utah, at the foot of the Bear River Mountains.

Marianne Hales Harding is a poet, essayist, and playwright. Her plays have been produced in theaters from New York to Seattle and she was the Playwright in Residence at the Utah Shakespeare Festival. Her work has been adapted for film by independent filmmakers and published by Brooklyn Publishers, Silver Birch Press, *Everyday Mormon Writer*, *ePregnancy* and *Rocky Mountain Running Magazine* (among others). She received her MFA in Playwriting from Ohio University and her BA in English from Brigham Young University. She is the co-founder of Speak for Yourself, a creative writing open mic and writing community in Provo, Utah.

Dianne Hardy lives with her cat, Aura, in Logan, Utah. She is a retired university professor who chooses to write, rather than stagnate in front of the television screen. In her younger days she made raw rebellion. Now she couches it in satire, which is equally effective. She is the author of *For Cryin' Out Loud!*, a memoir of her childhood.

Kimberly Johnson is a poet, translator, and Renaissance scholar. Her collections of poetry include, most recently, *Uncommon Prayer*, and her work has appeared in *The New Yorker*, *Slate*, and *Ploughshares*. Recipient of fellowships and awards from the Guggenheim Foundation and the National Endowment for the Arts, she lives in Salt Lake City, Utah.

Kase Johnstun lives and writes in Ogden, Utah. He is the author of *Beyond the Grip of Craniosynostosis* (McFarland & Co.), which was recently awarded the Gold Quill in Creative Nonfiction by the League of Utah Writers for 2015. Johnstun is the co-editor/author of *Utah Reflections: Stories from the Wasatch Front* (The History Press), which was named the Salt Lake Tribune's book of the month for August 2014 and the League of Utah Writers Recommended Read in Nonfiction 2015. His essay collection *Tortillas for Honkies* was named a finalist for the 2013 Autumn House press Nonfiction Awards (most of the essays in the collection have found homes in places like *The Watershed Review*, *Label Me Latino/a*, *Prime Number Literary Magazine*, and *Animal Literary Magazine*).

Tim Keller is a former president of the League of Utah Writers and is currently the president of the League's Cache Valley Chapter. The only thing he likes better than reading a good story is telling one. Tim always wanted to try his hand at writing, so a couple of years ago he began work on the Great American Novel. The ensuing obsession changed his life. He's since branched out into short prose and essays. He even works on the novel from time to time.

Maria Melendez Kelson published *Flexible Bones* (2010) and *How Long She'll Last in This World* (2006) with University of Arizona Press. Her books have been finalists for the Colorado Book Award and the PEN Center USA Poetry award. Her poetry and essays appear in *Poetry* magazine, *Ms.* magazine, *Sojourns*, and elsewhere. Her novel-in-progress, a mystery set in the redwood country of northern California, received the 2014 Eleanor Taylor Bland Crime Fiction Writers of Color Award from Sisters in Crime. She teaches literature and writing at Pueblo Community College. Find her on Twitter: @MKelsonAuthor.

Kate Kingston has published two books of poetry, *History of Grey*, a runner-up in the Main Street Rag Award and *Shaking the Kaleidoscope*, a finalist in the Idaho Prize. Her manuscript, *Motheresque*, placed finalist in the 2015 May Swenson Award. Kingston the recipient of the W.D Snodgrass Award for Poetic Endeavor and Excellence, the Ruth Stone Prize, and the Atlanta Review International Publication Prize.

John Kippen is a founding editor of the poetry magazine, *Sugar House Review*. He is currently exploring a casual interest in meditation and origami.

Lance Larsen, poet laureate of Utah, has published four poetry collections, most recently *Genius Loci* (Tampa 2013). He has received a number of awards, including a Pushcart Prize and a fellowship from the National Endowment for the Arts. He teaches at BYU where he coordinates the MFA program. He and his wife, Jacqui Larsen (a mixed-media artist), recently collaborated on a show titled *Three-Mile Radius*.

Joel Long's Winged Insects won the White Pine Press Poetry Prize. His *Knowing Time by Light* and *Lessons in Disappearance* were published by Blaine Creek Press. Chapbooks, *Chopin's Preludes* and *Saffron Beneath Every Frost* were published from Elik Press. His poems appeared in *Bitter Oleander, Interim, Massachusetts Review, Gulf Coast* among other journals.

Amanda Luzzader holds the office of Past President for the League of Utah Writers. She is an aspiring novelist and short story writer. Most recently her work can be found in the anthologies *It Came from the Great Salt Lake* and the *League of Utah Writers Anthology*. Among Amanda's other publications are several stories published in Chicken Soup for the Soul books and the anthologies *Old Scratch and Owl Hoots* and *In the Shimmering*. She is a technical and grant writer for a non-profit organization. Amanda enjoys reading, photography, and watching *Downton Abbey*.

Brittney McDonald is a Cache Valley native and is in her junior year at Utah State University, studying Creative Writing and American Studies. She is Vice President of her campus's creative writing club, a founding editor of the online undergraduate literary magazine *Sink Hollow*, and has poetry published in local collections and broadsides. When she isn't writing or reading, Brittney enjoys petting her dog and daydreaming about the zombie apocalypse.

Michael McLane is an editor for *Sugar House Review* and *saltfront: studies in human habit(at)*. He holds an MFA in Creative Writing from Colorado State University, and an MS in Environmental Humanities from the University of Utah. His own work has appeared in numerous journals, including *High Country News, Western Humanities Review, Colorado Review, Denver Quarterly*, and *Interim*. He lives in Salt Lake City where he is the Literary Program Officer for Utah Humanities and the director of the Utah Humanities Book Festival.

Dinty W. Moore is author of *Dear Mister Essay Writer Guy: Advice and Confessions on Writing, Love, and Cannibals* as well as the memoir *Between Panic & Desire*, winner of the Grub Street Nonfiction Book Prize. Moore has published essays and stories in *The Southern Review, The Georgia Review, Harpers, The New York Times Sunday Magazine, The Philadelphia Inquirer Magazine*, and *The Normal School* among numerous other venues. He edits *Brevity*, an online journal of flash nonfiction, and he is deathly afraid of polar bears.

Tessa Nicolaides graduated from Utah State University in English, with an emphasis in Creative Writing. She performed her flash non-fiction piece, "Air," at Helicon West in November of 2014. Tessa lives in Salt Lake City and works at The Road Home, the largest homeless shelter in Utah. She is super grateful for the experiences she had in the Utah State University English program.

Dániel Nyikos got his PhD in English from the University of Nebraska at Lincoln. He was born in Germany to a mother who grew up in Hungary and a father of Hungarian descent who grew up in the USA. In 2013-2014, he spent a year in Hungary with a Fulbright grant doing research for a novel. He currently lives in Hungary, where he teaches at the University of Szeged. In his free time, he enjoys writing, reading, and talking about reading and writing.

Márton "Storm Cleaver" Nyikos first burst on the scene in 1980 with the hit "Ride Me Like a Motorbike." After touring with Judas Priest, he developed a few bad habits, but now he's clean and runs a private no-kill shelter for Wookiees on his expansive ranch, which he shares with his wife Liz. The pair met while on a mission to Mordor that he still can't discuss.

Susan (Nyikos) Pesti-Strobel hails from Hungary. Her poems have been published in the annual chapbooks of her beloved poetry group, Poetry@3, the *wordriver anthology, ProvoOremWord, Sugar House*, and *Loose Leaves* (UK). She was a finalist for the Writers@Work fellowship competition in 2014. She also won a scholarship to the Summer Fishtrap writers' workshop in 2014. Susan has taught and judged poetry for the League of Utah Writers and judged poetry for the USU Scribendi creative writing contest. Though she lives in Oregon now, she was there when Helicon West started on the USU Logan campus, and hopes the program will thrive for many years to come.

Phil Parisi is a poet, painter, and writer living in Logan, Utah. His book of translations of poems of the Italian Resistance by Alfonso Gatto was published in 2011 (*The Wall Did Not Answer*, Chelsea Editions).

Charles Potts has authored a dozen books and has published books by thirty other poets. He was the editor/publisher of *Litmus* and *The Temple* magazines. *The Malpais Review*, a quarterly from Placitas, New Mexico, recently published his critical work on Charles Olson and Edward Dorn. He has donated his literary archive to the Merrill-Cazier Library at Utah State University in Logan, Utah. Potts has been publishing since 1963.

Alyssa Quinn is a recent graduate of the creative writing program at Utah State University. She has performed with the Bull Pen Creative Writing Club at numerous Helicon West events. Her work has appeared in *Brevity*, *Sweet*, *So to Speak*, and *The Claremont Review*, and in 2015 her flash fiction took first place in the League of Utah Writers' annual contest. Apart from writing, she loves hiking, *Star Trek*, and all things chocolate. In the fall of 2016 she will begin a creative writing MFA program at Western Washington University.

Jack Remick is a novelist and poet. He is the author of the novels *Blood* and *Gabriela and The Widow* (a finalist for the Montaigne Medal and Foreword Magazine Book of the Year Award). He has two poetry collections—*Satori*, and *The Seattle Five Plus One*. His work also includes two short story collections—*Terminal Weird*, and *Throwback and Other Stories*, as well as The California Quartet: *The Deification*, *Valley Boy*, *The Book of Changes*, and *Trio of Lost Soul*. He is co-author of *The Weekend Novelist Writes a Mystery* with Robert J. Ray.

Felicia Rose is a writer living in Cache Valley, Utah. Her work has appeared in *The Sun*, *The Change Agent*, *In Transit* and other publications. Currently, she writes for *Mother Earth News*.

Jordon Roberts graduated from Utah State University in 2015 with her bachelor's degree in creative writing. She enjoys writing all types of genres, but her main focuses lie in slam poetry and creative flash nonfiction. Jordon has performed at several slam poetry venues, including *WhySlam*, *Bull Pen Flash*, and *Kentucky's National Wild Women of Slam* competition where she took third place. She has been involved with Helicon West for three years and has presented her work at Helicon on several occasions. When she is not writing, her hobbies include working as a massage therapist, coloring, and taking road trips.

Born and raised in Seattle, ***Lisa Roullard*** earned her MFA in Creative Writing at Eastern Washington University. Her poetry has appeared in various magazines, including *Brain, Child*; *New Orleans Review*; and *Literal Latte*. Her work has also appeared on busses in Boise, Idaho, as part of Poetry in Motion. In 2013 she won the Utah Original Writing Competition for poetry. Lisa lives in Salt Lake City with her family, a trio of book lovers. As often as possible she walks in the rain.

Carrie Farmer Scheidel is thrilled to be included in this anthology. She has previously been published in *Sugar House Review* and *Lamplighter Review*. She has long worked as a Technical Writer, but is transitioning to communications for wildlife conservation, as she can't live in a world without elephants. She is also anxious to advocate for bats, bees, and bonobos. She would champion tardigrades, but they'll never need it. She enjoys watching football and *Jeopardy!* with her wife, two cats, and senior beagle.

Anne Shifrer's bird poems "Dippers" and "white robin" reflect her sojourn with the Audubon society and learning to watch birds in a more minute and appreciative manner.

Jennifer Sinor is the author of two forthcoming books. Her memoir, *Ordinary Trauma*, is a series of linked flash nonfiction, while *Letter Like the Day: On Reading Georgia O'Keeffe* is a collection of lyric pieces that move in, out, and beyond the literary art of one of America's first modernists. She has read from both projects at Helicon. Jennifer teaches creative writing at Utah State University where she is a professor of English. She lives in Logan, Utah, with her husband, poet Michael Sowder, and their two boys.

Jace Raymond Smellie is in the final year of his BA in Creative Writing at Utah State University. He grew up in the sagebrush hills of southeastern Idaho, but he considers anywhere from Idaho to Arizona as home. He holds a life-long passion for all forms of writing. His most current project is writing and directing a radio sit-com titled, "On the Quad," and he works on the USU college radio station's board of directors. In his rare spare time away from school, work, and his writing desk, he plays in competitive disc golf tournaments.

Michael Sowder's writing explores themes of wilderness, fatherhood, and spirituality. His first poetry collection, *The Empty Boat*, was chosen by Diane Wakoski to win the 2004 T.S. Eliot Award. His most recent collection, *House Under the Moon* (2012), combines poems of devotion to a feminine divine with poems about fatherhood. In 2014 he lived with his family in India as a Fulbright Fellow. His work has appeared in Ted Kooser's *American Life in Poetry*, *Five Points*, *Green Mountains Review*, *Poet Lore*, *Sufi Journal*, *New Poets of the American West*, *Pilgrimage*, *The New York Times Online*, *Shambhala Sun*, and elsewhere.

Laura Stott is the author of the book of poems, *In the Museum of Coming and Going* (New Issues Poetry & Prose, 2014). She received her M.F.A. from Eastern Washington University. Her poems can be found publications such as *Copper Nickel*, *Bellingham Review*, *Hayden's Ferry Review*, *Cutbank*, *Sugarhouse Review*, *Redactions*, and *Rock and Sling*. She loves to collaborate with other artists, including her "Blue Nude" poetry/painting series, with her sister, Katheryn Stott. Outside of poems, Laura spends as much time as possible with her family in their garden or the mountains of Utah. She is an Instructor of English at Weber State University.

Nathaniel Taggart is a founding editor of *Sugar House Review* and is proud to serve as annual fund manager at the Utah Shakespeare Festival as well as board member and webmaster of the Cedar City Arts Council. You can see some of his other work in places like *Diagram, Weber: The Contemporary West*, and *Kolob Canyon Review*.

Nancy Takacs is the 2016 winner of the Juniper Prize for poetry, her collection *The Worrier* to be published by the U. of Massachusetts Press in 2017. She has two other books of poems, including *Blue Patina* published in 2015 by Blue Begonia Press; and four chapbooks, one of which, *Red Voice*, will be published in 2016 from Finishing Line Press. Her poems have recently been published in the *Harvard Review, terrain.org, Hayden's Ferry Review*, and *Kestrel*. Nancy lives in Wellington, Utah.

Natalie Taylor earned a BFA in English with a creative writing emphasis from the University of Utah. She is the author of the poetry chapbook, *Eden's Edge*, published by Finishing Line Press in 2014. Taylor's poem, "Last Day of July," published in *Ellipsis, Literature and Art*, was a co-winner of the 2000 Academy of American Poets Contest. Her poetry has been published in *Brain, Child*.

Isaac Timm is a recent graduate of Utah State University; he holds Bachelor's Degrees in History and English Creative Writing. He lives in Logan with his wife Aaron. His poetry is inspired by the vast landscape of his childhood, the Western Desert of Utah, its distances and characters.

William Trowbridge's graphic chapbook, *Oldguy: Superhero*, will be published by Red Hen Press in March. His new full collection, *Tilt-A-Whirl*, is forthcoming from Red Hen in 2017. His other collections are *Put This On, Please: New and Selected Poems, Ship of Fool, The Complete Book of Kong, Flickers, O Paradise*, and *Enter Dark Stranger*. He teaches in the University of Nebraska low-residency MFA in writing program and is currently Poet Laureate of Missouri.

Millie Tullis is a student at Utah State University, and was allowed her first opportunity to perform at Helicon West. She won first place in the Sandy River Review's undergraduate poetry contest in 2015. She hopes to get an MFA in poetry and a PhD in creative writing and teach creative writing.

Stephen Tuttle lives in Provo, Utah and teaches at Brigham Young University. His fiction has appeared in *The Gettysburg Review, Black Warrior Review, Hayden's Ferry Review, The Normal School*, and elsewhere.

Jerry VanIeperen lives in Utah with his wife and two children. He briefly considered writing manifestos from a dark, windowless cabin in the heart of the

Rocky Mountains, but felt his beard was not quite Nordic enough for such endeavors. He received an MFA from the University of Nebraska and is a founding editor of the poetry journal *Sugar House Review*.

Chadd VanZanten, co-author of *On Fly-Fishing the Northern Rockies: Essays and Dubious Advice*, is on a fishing trip.

Charles Waugh lives in the mountain town of Logan, Utah, where he teaches at Utah State University. With Nguyen Lien and Van Gia, he is the co-editor and co-translator of *Wild Mustard: New Voices from Viet Nam*, a collection of nineteen short stories from young Vietnamese writers forthcoming from Curbstone Press in 2017. He and Lien are also co-editors and co-translators of *Family of Fallen Leaves, Stories of Agent Orange by Vietnamese Writers*, available from the University of Georgia Press.

Travis Williams was born and raised in Utah. He loves baseball, peanut butter and jelly, Walt Whitman, and Logan, Utah.

With a major in English, emphasis in Creative Writing, and a minor in Psychology, *Jeannie Woller* spends her time studying how the mind can connect with the voice in order to highlight individual and shared experiences. A three-year member of her school's indie Slam Poetry team, a finalist in the Wild Women of Poetry Slam National competition through the University of Kentucky Women's Conference, as well as a 4 year member of her University's D1 Women's soccer team, this will be her first publication.

Harald Wyndham is a poet and the owner of Blue Scarab Press, which has published over twenty-four titles by Southeast Idaho and regional writers since 1984. He lives with his wife, Jane, in Pocatello, Idaho.

Natalie Young is a founding editor for the poetry magazine *Sugar House Review*. By day, she works as an art director for an ad agency based in Salt Lake City. Previous publications include *Los Angeles Times, Rattle, South Dakota Review, Tampa Review, Green Mountains Review*, and others. She is a fan of Dolly Parton and Swiss cheese.

Native of Utah, *Shari Zollinger* has a BS in History from Utah State University. She spent six years of her life living in Taiwan, part of that time spent attending the Stanford Inter-University Program for Chinese Language Studies in Taipei. Her love travel has directly inspired her work as a poet. Her poems have appeared in the *Sugar House Review, Redactions: Poetry and Poetics*, and *The Desert Voice*. She is currently working on a manuscript inspired by the works of Auguste Rodin.

ACKNOWLEDGEMENTS

Ballam, Shanan. "Grandmother Waiting for Red Riding Hood: The Footprint" published in *burntdistrict*; "Wolf Wears Red Riding Hood's Cape" published in *Crab Orchard Review*; "Red Riding Hood and Her Mother: The City" published in *Sugar House Review*.

Beck, Russ. "America's Caveat River" published in *On Fly-Fishing the Northern Rockies: Essays and Dubious Advice*, The History Press, 2015.

Cokinos, Christopher "You searched for: *elegy*, then for *ode*" published in *Blackbox Manifold*, formerly titled "commutation" and published in *Held as Earth*.

Coles, Katharine. "The Double Leash" and "A Confusion" published in *Poetry*; "Dog Days," "Dog Years," "A Dog in Time," and "Cleo at Fourteen" published in *Able Muse*; "San Marco's Floors," published in *Flight*, Red Hen Press, 2016.

Coulbrooke, Star. "Sky's the Limit" published in *Redactions: Poetry and Poetics*, Issue 13.

Dethier, Brock. "The Wart Doctor Makes a House Call," published in *Reclamation*, Popcorn Press, 2015.

Dixon, Cat. "Last Testament in Snow," and "The Illness" published in *Eva*, Stephen F Austin University Press, 2016.

Frost, Heather. "The Truest Character" published in *Asides: A Short Story Collection*, 2014.

Griffiths, Siân. "The Most Natural Thing in the World" published in *Fifth Wednesday Journal*.

Gunsberg, Ben. "Machine Overheard Teaching Boy to Read" published in *The Bad Penny Review*.

Hardy, Dianne. "Lot" published in *Parody Magazine*.

Johnson, Kimberly. "Farthingale" and "Freefall" published in *Crazyhorse* 85.

Keller, Tim. "The Gift" published in *Words to Paint With: A Collection of Prose and Poetry*, LUW Press, 2012.

Luzzader, Amanda. "Between Places" published in *Between Places*, LUW Press, 2014.

McLane, Michael. "Sky, Falling" published in *Tuesday: An Art Project*. "Settlement" published in burntdistrict.

Nyikos, Daniel. "Potato Soup" published online in *American Life in Poetry*. Reprinted in *Being: What Makes a Man*, and in two projects by Pearson Publishing, "Senior Secondary English Series" and *Literature for Composition*.

Potts, Charles. "Sport Utility Poem" published in *Slash & Burn* from Blue Begonia Press in Yakima, Washington. Reprinted in *High Country News*.

Sinor, Jennifer. "Holes in the Sky" published in *Seneca Review*. Forthcoming in *Letters Like the Day: Reading Georgia O'Keeffe*, University of New Mexico Press, 2017.

Sowder, Michael. "Former Attorney" published in *The Empty Boat*, T.S. Eliot Prize, New Odyssey Series, 2004; "Learning Names" published in *Southern Poetry Review*; "Aidan Looks at the Moon" and "Kellen in my Lap" published in *Poetry Kanto*.

Stott, Laura. "The Fall" and "The girl with no hands" published in *In the Museum of Coming and Going*, New Issues Poetry and Prose, 2014.

Taggart, Nathaniel. "Our Love and Some Objects," Urban Design: The City of Zion Platt," and "We Dream and Believe the Rest to be True" published in *15 Bytes*.

Trowbridge, William. "Proof of Intelligent Life," "Obedience," and "Mr. Fixit" published in *Put This On, Please: New and Selected Poems*, Red Hen Press, 2014.

Tuttle, Stephen. "The Scold" published online, as part of the 7 Days, 7 Artists, 7 Rings project on *The Huffington Post*.

VanIeperen, Jerry. "Unsaught Baptisms and a Broken Coffee Pot" published in *burntdistrict*.

Waugh, Charles. "The Folly of Crows" published in *The Platte Valley Review* 31.1.

Wyndham, Harald. "East of Missoula" and "One Last Voyage Round the Horn" published in *the Same Moon Shines on us All*, Poems 2004-2015, Blue Scarab Press, 2015.

Young, Natalie. "Dirty Yellow Blanket" published in *Journal of Pedagogy, Pluralism and Practice*.

ABOUT THE EDITORS

Chadd VanZanten has been active in Helicon West activities for many years and is thrilled to be a small part of making this anthology a reality. Chadd was active in the conception, fundraising, and marketing efforts for the book, and he assisted with selecting the content.

Tim Keller is a long time member of the Helicon West planning committee and considers Helicon a secret too good to keep. He is delighted to have played a role in the creation of this, the first ever Helicon West anthology, and is proud to be a member of the acquisitions, marketing and production teams.

Star Coulbrooke would like to thank Chadd and Tim for pitching the book proposal and handling the details that made its production seem possible. She also extends her gratitude to the authors who gave generously of their time and talent to read for Helicon West and contribute their work to the anthology. She takes full responsibility for editing and formatting, with apologies for any omissions or errors in the book.

www.ingramcontent.com/pod-product-compliance
Lightning Source LLC
Chambersburg PA
CBHW020646260626
47157CB00008B/2922